To Edward [?]

With very best wishes,

Craig

Mannerism and *Maniera*

INSTITUTE OF FINE ARTS, NEW YORK UNIVERSITY

Mannerism and *Maniera*

CRAIG HUGH SMYTH

J. J. AUGUSTIN PUBLISHER, LOCUST VALLEY, NEW YORK

TO

BARBARA LINFORTH SMYTH

Preface

This book comprises a paper read in the session on "Recent Concepts of Mannerism" at the Twentieth International Congress of Art Historians in September, 1961, and footnotes to it. As given at the Congress, the paper was limited to thirty minutes. As printed, it is twice as long, but the lecture form has been kept. The paper is also being published in its long version in the *Acts* of the Congress, but without footnotes, since the full text and notes together are too extensive for the *Acts*.

I hope that the paper will be read first by itself without the notes, so that the main argument may emerge unencumbered. The notes give support for statements in the text, deal with the literature on Mannerism, where much of the subject's complexity originates, and also touch problems in the development of Renaissance painting that are related to the problem of Mannerism.

The treatment of Mannerism presented here developed from my dissertation, *Bronzino Studies*, Princeton University, 1955, and from a public lecture given first at Mount Holyoke College in February, 1956. The view of the stylistic relationship of *maniera* to Roman relief was suggested originally in a draft of the dissertation, submitted in 1953.

In planning the publication of the book, I have had from Millard Meiss, President of the Twentieth International Congress of Art Historians, and Ida E. Rubin, Executive Secretary of the Congress, advice and help that I appreciate greatly. I am particularly grateful to E. H. Gombrich, chairman of the session of the Congress in which the present paper was given, for several additions indicated in the footnotes; to Richard Krautheimer, Rensselaer Lee, and David Allan Robertson, Jr., who have given me helpful comments on the manuscript; and to Walter Friedlaender, from whose work I have learned so much and from whom I have had steady encouragement. It is a pleasure to record my special thanks to H. W. Janson, who has acted as editor for the book and, in particular, saved me from one error of interpretation. Much of the necessary study abroad was made possible by a Fulbright Fellowship and later by grants to the Institute of Fine Arts, New York University, from Robert Lehman, Lauder Greenway, and Mr. and Mrs. Charles B. Wrightsman, to all of whom I am profoundly grateful. I should like to express my gratitude to the Frick Art Reference Library, on which I have relied regularly for a long time. I am much indebted to Count and Countess Guglielmo Castelbarco Albani for permitting me to study the decorations in the Villa Imperiale at Pesaro and have photographs made there. To Naomi Miller I am grateful for help with references and photographs and for typing the manuscript originally, and I am obliged to Stephany Haines and Judith Levenson for typing revisions. Four people ably and uncomplainingly took on many of my daily chores from time to time, so that I could write: Robert Goldwater, Wolfgang Lotz, Clemencia Kessler, and Joanna Hill. My warmest thanks to them. My wife has helped with encouragement and acute observations on pictures. The book is gratefully and fondly dedicated to her.

Institute of Fine Arts
New York University

October, 1962

List of Illustrations

ix

We speak of Mannerism in many arts. Yet our concepts of it in each descend from the use of the word *maniera* long ago for something that had developed in Cinquecento painting. My aim is to examine again the way *maniera* was used and what development it referred to, so that we may compare our modern concepts of Mannerism. This is one way of testing them, as Ernst Gombrich proposes we should.[1] But, let me add, I do so only in relation to painting.

Present concepts of Mannerism owe much to contributions made thirty-five or forty years ago.[2] Of these, I want to mention at the outset the classic work on the anticlassical style by Walter Friedlaender,[3] who is here today. Given first as a lecture in 1914, it showed the singular originality of pictures like Pontormo's *Christ before Pilate* (Fig. 1) and taught us their strange beauty. Walter Friedlaender and others disclosed for the first time a great deal about Italian painting at Raphael's death that will stand our tests.

Now being questioned anew, however, are some of their explanations and definitions, and even the assumption that paintings like the *Christ before Pilate* are Mannerism. Although not widely shared, this doubt, expressed by Mario Salmi and a few others, keeps nagging.[4] Walter Friedlaender himself was not satisfied with the term for such painting. He used it, but preferred the name "anticlassical style," because, as he explained, it ran counter to the High Renaissance, which to us is classic, or classical.[5] Hermann Voss hung back, preferring the general heading "Late Renaissance." In 1916,

I

Frederick M. Clapp wrote about Pontormo without using the word Mannerism. But this is not surprising, for at that moment the concept of Mannerism that had prevailed in the nineteenth century had scarcely begun to change. The nineteenth century's concept was based, as we know, on the seventeenth century's view of "la maniera" as a vice that had caused the decline of Cinquecento painting, the view that we find in Bellori, supported by Malvasia and others.[6]

To the nineteenth century, Mannerism in Italian painting had meant simply a decline that began in Florence and Rome after 1530 or '40 (Figs. 2 and 3), with some anticipations earlier. From Lanzi and Fiorillo through Müntz and Riegl this decline involved chiefly one thing: excessive adherence to a manner or manners full of unjustified habitual peculiarities, remote from nature, and due above all to three causes. The first cause was uncomprehending and mostly exclusive imitation of some previous style—that of Michelangelo principally, but in some cases of Raphael or Correggio, or of antique sculpture. (The main antecedent for this view was a concern about exclusive imitation voiced in the sixteenth, not the seventeenth century.[7]) Second was routine dexterity gained through practice, a dexterity that was mechanical and superficial because of haste and lack of knowledge. And the third was an admixture of extravagance and caprice.[8]

The decline was considered inevitable and involuntary. It was inevitable that artists should imitate an overpowering style like Michelangelo's and inevitable that decline should follow the early Cinquecento, when the problems of technique and composition had been solved—like a biological law, as Müntz thought.[9] Special conditions in Italy only encouraged it. The change in the status of artists from journeymen to courtiers led them to exchange serious study for pretentious display.[10] The demand for extensive, hasty decorations led them to be quick and superficial.[11] The tendency

2

in Italian art to generalize and idealize led them to neglect nature.[12] Only Riegl, to my knowledge, explicitly tried to find a positive artistic purpose; he decided it might be to achieve a decorative effect of lines and colors.[13]

This bare statement is enough to remind us how new were the concepts that developed in the twentieth century after Riegl. Under the influence of modern expressionism and abstraction[14] (and the idea that their revolt against nature stemmed from a new spirituality[15]) Mannerism was transformed. Another aspect of Seicento opinion was taken up: the view that "la maniera" depended on imagination working without regard for truth to nature or the example of previous masters and antiquity.[16] And in the process the date of Mannerism's full emergence was moved back to 1520 and earlier.[17] Introduced as the focal point of the problem were works of the 'twenties by Pontormo (Fig. 1), Rosso, Beccafumi, and Parmigianino that had scarcely been connected with Mannerism before, also the work of El Greco and, with less agreement, the later paintings of Michelangelo.[18] With these as a basis, Mannerism became a laudable style,[19] and the familiar chain of conclusions developed: that it aimed at a new aesthetic and a disquieting expressiveness, was in rebellion against the High Renaissance and ideal naturalness, hence "anticlassical," a deviation from the classic norm, hence abnormal (recently it has even been compared to surrealism), and that it was rooted in the spiritual unrest of its age.[20] This is the principal trend of opinion, although some have disagreed—Weisbach for one[21]—and there are other less dominant concepts, which we shall consider briefly later.

But when Mannerism acquired its new implications, it retained the old nineteenth century meaning partly intact. What had been Mannerism before—Vasari's *Immaculate Conception* or Bronzino's *Saint Lawrence* (Figs. 2 and 3)—now became mature, academic, or later Mannerism; and the style it uncomprehendingly imitated became the Mannerism of

3

the 1520's.[22] The notion of an involuntary decline toward mid-century remained, though it grew fainter.

The two meanings have not been easy to reconcile. Objections have been raised to the term Mannerism for Pontormo and also for Rosso.[23] To classify works like Vasari's and Bronzino's, the droll name "mannered Mannerism" has been useful.[24]

But the difficulties go deeper then terminology.[25] Both the nineteenth and twentieth century components of the prevailing view make it difficult to look clearly at the Cinquecento. For both were based on statements about "la maniera" made in the seventeenth century, when taste had already changed; and in each a new slant was given: in the first instance by the nineteenth century's heavy stress on uncomprehending imitation (a concern of the sixteenth rather than the seventeenth century, as mentioned before, but not one voiced regarding the fundamentals of *maniera* as we shall see it);[26] in the second instance by interpretations depending on modern experience.

*   *   *

Dolce[27] says, in the mid-sixteenth century, that painters of his day—quite likely Venetians, since Dolce tells it—were using the word *maniera* derogatively in connection with painting in which one saw forms, faces, and (by implication) movements that were "almost always alike." In the passage in question Dolce praises Raphael because in his painting, he says, "one figure does not resemble another either in bearing or movement; hence, there is not a shadow in it of what is derogatively called by painters today *maniera*, namely, bad practice where forms and faces almost always look alike ("... in ciò non appare ombra di quello che da' pittori oggi in mala parte è chiamata maniera, cioè cattiva pratica, ove si veggono forme e volti quasi sempre simili"). In short, in the opinion of certain contemporary painters, *maniera* was monotonously uniform in respect to figures.

We classify Vasari's painting as typical of mature Mannerism. To judge from what he wrote in both the first and second editions of his *Lives*, he believed in a uniform ideal for figures, in painting in general, it would seem, and thought this the basis of *bella maniera*. In the introduction of Part III of the *Lives*,[28] Vasari states that *maniera* had been added to painting on its way to sixteenth century perfection. "*La maniera*," he continues, "became *la più bella* from the method of copying frequently the most beautiful things,[29] combining them to make from what was most beautiful (whether hands, heads, bodies, or legs) the best figure possible, *and putting it into use in every work for all the figures*—from this it is said comes *bella maniera*" (". . .e metterla in uso in ogni opera per tutte le figure; che per questo si dice esser bella maniera"). The idea of *imitare*, as against *ritrarre*,[30] is pushed here to a logical, if tiresome, conclusion.

What Dolce connected with *maniera* and did not like and Vasari connected with *maniera*, particularly *bella maniera*, and praised, is pertinent to the problem of Mannerism and should be brought to bear on it.[31] The use of the term *maniera* reported by Dolce ought to interest us particularly. It has a good claim to be the direct antecedent of the Seicento use,[32] from which subsequent concepts of Mannerism stemmed. For it is derogatory like Bellori's and in all probability refers to the same type of Cinquecento painting.

Malvasia names as painters who worked in an entirely *manieroso* way Vasari, Salviati, the Zuccari, Andrea Vicentino, Tomaso Laureti, "and, of our [Bolognese painters], Samacchini, Sabbatini, Calvaert, the Procaccini and the like."[33] To judge from the context of Bellori's use of the word *maniera*,[34] he, too, must have meant such painters as these when he told how the vice of *maniera* became rooted. In the work of Vasari and the others, and of painters like them, uniformity of forms, faces, bearing, and movement is more striking than in any other kind of Cinquecento painting, as nineteenth century criticism emphasized. Dolce's *maniera* must have had reference above all to their sort of work. On his testimony the word *maniera* was connected derogatively with such painting almost from the outset, by artists who were critical of it.

Dolce's *maniera* promises us help: its meaning is not yet subject to Seicento taste, and Vasari's *maniera* and *bella maniera* elucidate it as having a slighting reference to the meaning Vasari gives.[35] Moreover, neither Dolce's meaning nor Vasari's appears to be cancelled by other implications of the word current in the Cinquecento. On the contrary, Dolce's *maniera* probably carries some of these implications.

There is no reason to suppose that Dolce gave all the overtones of the derogatory use of *maniera* in his brief reference to it.[36] Since it alluded to monotonous reliance on the same forms, faces, and movements, doubtless it already implied a tendency not to refer back to nature, or reality, sufficiently.[37] For the same reason, it must already have been closely related to the notion of reliance on *pratica*, which implied routine usage as well as the practised hand. Dolce himself links the two words.[38] Weise has indicated that, in reference to polite society, *maniera* had long referred to purposeful artificiality in deportment.[39] Possibly Dolce's *maniera* implied artificiality in paintings like Vasari's.[40] But, for that matter, Dolce's *maniera* could hardly have failed to call to mind, in some degree, the striking features of style that prevailed throughout the painting thus labeled, whether or not disapproval extended to all these features. (To the extent that it did call them to mind, the use of *maniera* reported by Dolce could have served, practically, as a designation for a trend in style—a disparaging designation.)

6

But there is no suggestion that Dolce thought of *maniera* as based mainly on capricious imagination.[41] Nor does Vasari suggest that he himself thought so.[42] This appears to be a later view, first explicitly stated in the seventeenth century.[43]

In the seventeenth century, opinion solidified against Cinquecento *maniera*, not just against its uniformity and routine, but against the whole ideal of beauty that painters had purveyed so uniformly and routinely. To Bellori, Malvasia, and Agucchi, Cinquecento *maniera* was simply fantastic. Taste had changed completely.[44]

* * *

In the introduction to Part III of the *Lives*, Vasari[45] lists the qualities missing in painting before about 1500 and then enumerates the successive contributions to painting in the modern sixteenth century style, from its inauguration by Leonardo down to its perfection in Vasari's day. This is Vasari's summary of the development of Cinquecento painting. It is helpful to keep it in mind, because it gives the development from a mid-century vantage point and suggests something of what Vasari himself aimed for in painting. It suggests, too, something of what he asked of an ideal figure that could be used "for all the figures."[46]

Among the qualities wanting before the sixteenth century, Vasari put first *licenzia*: "nella regola una licenzia," "within the rule, license, which, while not being according to rule, might be ordered within the rule . . . without making confusion or spoiling the order." There follow: "abundant invention in everything," "a certain beauty continued in every smallest thing," and grace in the figures that depends on judgment and transcends mere measurement.[47] Grace, which is much stressed, has overtones of sweetness, lightness, and refine-

7

ment, as in the following items: "a graceful, sweet facility" in doing muscles; ". . . all the figures svelte and graceful . . ."; the fleshy members not "rude as in nature but refined by draftsmanship and judgment." Other lacks of the Quattrocento were: "abundance in beautiful garments"; "variety of bizarre fancies"; "loveliness of colors"; and "finish and utmost perfection in feet, hands, hair, and beards"—*minuzie dei fini*. Because of too much study, painting had been dry and harsh; attempting the impossible, it had lacked liveliness — *uno spirito di prontezza*.

Newly found antiquities influenced the improvement of painting at the end of the Quattrocento. It was these "in their sweetness and in their severities," as Vasari says, "with their *termini carnosi* . . ., with certain actions that do not involve twisting contortions throughout but movement in certain parts" and have the greatest grace, that brought finish and the elimination of dryness and crudeness.

Among the successive contributions to the modern manner, from the end of the Quattrocento to Vasari's day and leading to perfection in his time, were: the new unified sweetness in colors (*dolcezza ne' colori unita*) begun by Francia and Perugino; Leonardo's vigor and boldness in *disegno* (*gagliardezza e bravezza del disegno*), his "subtle simulation of all nature's minutiae," and the movement and breath in his figures; then, Raphael's harvest of the best from all sources[48] to achieve the "perfection of Apelles' and Zeuxis' figures . . . and more"; Raphael's contribution of easy invention that made his history pictures "like writings" with their circumstantial detail;[49] the grace of Raphael's heads; Correggio's contribution of soft, feathery hair; Parmigianino's improvements on Correggio in grace, ornaments, and *bella maniera* (one ideal figure for all the figures, by Vasari's definition); Polidoro's and Maturino's gestures and inventions in façade pictures, their truth to Roman antiquity, the *pratica* and dexterity of their execution; and the life that Rosso, Sebas-

8

tiano del Piombo, Giulio Romano, and Perino del Vaga gave to their figures in color.

Thanks to these and other painters, the art of painting at mid-century was at last, Vasari says, "so perfect and easy for anyone having *disegno*, invention, and coloring" that Vasari and his contemporaries, he was glad to state, could paint six panels in one year where their own masters did one in six.[50]

But transcending and enveloping all was the contribution of Michelangelo, which Vasari defined elsewhere as opening "the road to painting's facility in its principal object, the human body."[51] He far surpassed the ancients in both sculpture and painting: compared with them in respect to heads, hands, arms, and feet he had a "sounder foundation, a grace more completely graceful, and a much more absolute perfection, carried through with a certain difficulty that is so easy...one cannot see better." At the same time, Michelangelo had set the "ultimate limit" for all three arts.

To judge from this account, Vasari thought painting at its peak in his time. Even if his concepts of "the ultimate limit" and of the biological growth and decay of art, as he expressed it elsewhere, made him think of the possibility of future decline, he viewed painting at mid-century with satisfaction.[52]

*　　*　　*

The monotony of figures that Dolce's painters referred to scornfully with the word *maniera* was not, in the work of Vasari and others like him, simply a matter of using the same forms, faces, and movements. Behind it was something more fundamental: the more or less consistent application of principles that governed form and movement—principles of posing figures at rest or in motion and of delineating, lighting, and grouping them. It is striking how uniformly they were applied and how inescapable is their effect on the eye.

9

"Habits," "formulae," "conventions" are words they always bring to mind and, equally, the word "peculiarities." Ever since the seventeenth century, at least, they have seemed odd.

The mid-Cinquecento conventions of the figure, as I shall call them, have drawn the attention of a number of critics. Weisbach, Voss, Dvořák, Pinder, Pevsner, Antal, and others have brought out aspects of them.[53] In the painting of the artists on Malvasia's list and of many of their contemporaries the conventions of the figure dominate, to a greater or lesser degree. The more they do, the more the term *maniera* appears to be in order, for they are the very basis of the monotony criticized in Dolce's use of *maniera*. One ideal figure for all figures was not literally attainable in the Cinquecento,[54] and in any case we know that a more or less uniform ideal has not necessarily meant monotony in other periods. Monotony here came especially from the context of conventions in which the ideal was presented. The impression not only of routine, but also of inattention to reality and of artificiality goes back principally to them. But as I shall stress, none of these conventions was wholly new.

If we want a clear view of them, we must look at extreme examples, from the work of Vasari and those like him. Most conspicuous is the tendency to flatten figures parallel to the picture plane (Figs. 2 to 9), especially the more noticeable figures, whether in foreground or distance. At the same time, poses are often abruptly twisted in two and three directions. The figure that seems flat, and yet turns, moves in depth, or is foreshortened, is characteristic. As Pinder saw, the impression is of forced flatness.

Indispensable support for this effect is given by flat light. This light is a hallmark of *maniera* and adds to its uniformity. For it tends, habitually, to belong to planes that parallel the picture plane. Shadow, on the other hand, is reserved chiefly for surfaces that recede or project. Armenini describes the method.[55] Moreover, whatever surface the flat light of *maniera* touches, this surface, flat or not, tends to look flat, until one pauses to analyze it. So great is the importance of limbs in *maniera*[56] that if only one arm or leg is flat, or flatly lighted, this is enough to suggest flatness far beyond it. Painters like Bronzino (Fig. 5), who experimented with three-dimensional poses, made use of this. Quite evidently they liked to exploit the strain between two and three dimensions, between restricting flatness and poses suggesting the need of freedom and flexibility. From this strain comes, I think, some of the sense of difficulty they valued in twisting and foreshortened figures.[57]

Only a little less insistent is the inclination to juxtapose figures side by side, or tangent to each other (Figs. 6, 7). Again the light helps, emphasizing separation. Where forms do overlap, confluence is avoided. The effect is achieved with draped figures as well as nude (Figs. 7, 8). Once more there is strain, between juxtaposition and the need for flow and fusion, which the earlier Cinquecento had felt strongly and supplied.

More pervasive are the principles of angularity and of spotting the composition with angular elements (Figs. 2 to 9).[58] Elongation is not central to *maniera*, but these two conventions are. On occasion bodies are bent in an angle at the waist to the point of dislocation (Fig. 3). Legs and arms are habitually bent (Figs. 2, 9). And they are placed where their pattern will tell, in short stiff shapes, generally diagonal. An arm held angularly across the chest (Fig. 5) or in the air (Fig. 19)[59] is almost a signature of *maniera*. Figures persistently take characteristic forms, which can be recorded in a diagrammatic shorthand of straight lines (Fig. 10),[60] and carry in themselves the agitated, broken, and unstable rhythms of *maniera* composition. No wonder that to the quick, unsympathetic eye the compositions of out-and-out *maniera* pictures tend to look alike, despite the premium that painters put upon inventiveness. In extremes the compositional units are the body's members—limbs, heads, torsos.

And as for composition, let us note, too, in passing that paintings with more than a few figures tend to lack a focal point, that secondary figures are apt to be abundant and more or less equally stressed in the uniform light, dispersing attention and obscuring the subject. Sometimes (Figs. 3, 9) it is as if painters sought obscurity with their vaunted copiousness and made an odd virtue out of the cross-purposes of composition and subject matter, just as they did out of unmotivated pose and movement (Fig. 5).[61]

There are also the conventions of delineating the figure, which are familiar and quickly listed. Boschini said Florentine draftmanship transformed live figures into statues,[62] and this applies generally to *maniera*. In refining nature's rudeness (as Vasari would say), *maniera* draftsmanship does not much want to record irregularities, plumb the inner structure, or show variety by making differentiations. In drawings, whether contours glide slowly and evenly (Fig. 11), or vibrate and are broken into segments (Fig. 12), they are habitually what van Mander found convenient but cursory[63] and Baldinucci insufficiently searching.[64] The same can be said of the smooth modeling of surfaces[65] (Figs. 4, 5, 11); sometimes the effect in painting is like that of some lifeless, uniform substance, not flesh and blood. What Malvasia called the "feeble washed-out" coloring also avoids the differentiation of nature, and this was not inadvertent. It was partly the purpose in coloring, Vasari and Armenini indicated, to avoid the contrasts of differentiation as lacking beauty and unity, as lacking "dolcezza ne' colori unita."[66] Line, modeling, and color were all better suited to serve a uniform ideal than nature's variety. And they were better suited, by the same token, to the accelerated production prized by Vasari than to laborious research. Indeed, this is true of all the conventions of the figure.

But finish and details, especially in the human figure, were important to Vasari and his contemporaries, as we saw.[67]

Finish in "feet, hands, hair, and beards" (Figs. 2, 3, 4, 5, 7, 8, 9)—evidently these extremities deserved special care as a locus of grace. Abundant garments and accoutrements (Figs. 7, 9)—to Vasari these were among the significant contributions to painting. To us, both seem rather strange in the stylized context of *maniera*. Of all the results of the Renaissance conquest of nature, the one that painters chose to cling to most was the "simulation of .... minutiae," owed, Vasari said, to Leonardo above all. Not that they sought special insight into detail. They were concerned with making it clear, polished, and refined, with imparting to foot, hand, hair, or beard something of *maniera* form and rhythm, with "a certain beauty continued in every smallest thing."[68] Neither thingness and uniqueness nor structure and function were primary. In drawings, of course, finish and minutiae were less often appropriate. There the rapid sketch prevailed, with its own strong tradition going back to Leonardo[69] (as Vasari's words seem to recognize).

Maniera painting is an art of figures, as most central Italians thought painting should be.[70] Space has not yet been mentioned. It can be deep (Fig. 3), or it can be shallow and almost eliminated (Fig. 7), just as in the early Pontormo. More important, the ground is habitually tilted upward, placing the rear figures higher (Figs. 3, 4, 8, 9, 13). And often one can describe the space as divided, or broken, into parts that are not easily grasped together (Figs. 3, 8, 13). More could be said; but these are the prime conventions of space, and in any case, as Dolce and Vasari indicated and we may repeat, *maniera*'s chief locus is the figure.

The conventions of *maniera* were employed sometimes with exaggerated refinement and elegance (Fig. 7), sometimes with exaggerated robustness and muscularity (Fig. 3). They were much played upon for extravagant and novel effects.[71] Within their context was often inserted a "variety of bizarre fancies" and poses.[72] Subjects were sometimes perplexingly complicated.[73] But it must have been the conventions them-selves that the seventeenth century objected to most of all as fantastic. We can surmise this because they were eliminated by seventeenth century painters, beginning with the Carracci and Caravaggio.

*　　*　　*

Where did the conventions of *maniera* come from? We can trace their beginnings earlier in painting, and later on I shall mention where. But one influence was surely antique relief.[74] It had to do with both the peculiarities of *maniera* and the preference for a uniform ideal—or monotony, as Dolce's painters considered it.

Roman sarcophagi of the second to fourth centuries (Figs. 14–18)—as described by Riegl,[75] for example—antic-ipate *maniera* in a number of ways: the flattening of figures (especially keeping both shoulders *en face*); their action in two dimensions; the isolation of principal figures and groups of figures from each other; the role of light and shade in emphasizing the separation; the way the forms catch the light; its flatness on their forward planes; the simplified contours and surfaces; the frequent emphasis on arms and legs and the system of linear composition, as Riegl saw it, with its stress on diagonals in the pattern of figures and limbs;[76] agitated movement; the lack of compositional focus; the surface patterns that have little to do with the action;[77] the "copiousness" in respect to figures;[78] and, by no means least, the impression that faces, forms, and movements are more or less alike. The message of the sarcophagi was rein-forced by Rome's two columns, by classicistic reliefs, coins, and sardonyx cameos, with their flat bright figures. The characteristics of the most available antique art prefigured the conventions of *maniera*. In *maniera*, their more extreme manifestations were followed, modernized, and exaggerated.

14

Critics of Cinquecento *maniera* in the Seicento, who so influenced later views, did not say that behind it lay antique relief. On the contrary, they spoke of its neglect of ancient art[79] and associated *maniera* and *ammanierato* with mere caprice. Perhaps the Seicento view of ancient art kept them from recognizing its role in *maniera*. But the Cinquecento was the time *par exellence* for feverish study of antiquities. Study of them was essential, Armenini explains, for gaining *maniera*.[80] The beginner, he says, learns more from copying "statues, [reliefs on] arches, and sarcophagi" than from anything else, because they "impress themselves on the mind by being more certain and true."[81] Painters draw sarcophagi so often because of "the copiousness and variety of beautiful things to be seen on them."[82] And the modern works to copy are the ones nearest ancient sculpture, starting with Polidoro's monochromes.[83] In Vasari's opinion, the only way to achieve *disegno* was to study nature, the best modern works, and antique relief.[84] Like Aretino, Vasari praised the "antiquely modern and modernly antique" in painting, and work of his own was praised in the same words.[85]

It is not surprising that the result in *maniera* went beyond the borrowing of antique poses to the principles of style.[86] But in contrast to strictly *all' antica* painting, *maniera* painting elaborated and, exactly as it was said, modernized them. Roman relief even affected what was done with space. David Coffin connects Ligorio's neglect of depth and perspective with his special interest in antiquities. Ligorio's, I think, is only a more archaeologically oriented case of a general phenomenon in *maniera* pictures and earlier.[87]

To document the antique-*maniera* relationship that I have suggested, Rosalind Grippi has studied the use of specific antique poses and gestures in *maniera* with good results, which she is preparing to publish.[88] They show that, besides general principles, *maniera* took antique poses and motifs on an extensive scale. Two of her examples will stand for many. The

Naples *Trapezophor*, then in Rome,[89] and figures like those on the lid of a Niobid sarcophagus in the Vatican[90] evidently lie behind the fallen soldiers of Bronzino's *Resurrection*.[91] They inspire both poses and pattern. The characteristic twisting *maniera* figures in Salviati's *David Refrains from Killing Saul*[92] and the almost exactly similar figure at the right of Bronzino's tapestry, *The Coming of Jacob into Egypt*,[93] instead of going back, as recently suggested, to late Gothic examples by artists like Multscher,[94] must come, Mrs. Grippi points out, from a Bacchic nymph like one to be seen on the Bacchic sarcophagi in the Walters Gallery[95] and at Naples.[96] Typically, Bronzino exaggerates the model. Such repetition of the same pose by both Bronzino and Salviati is characteristic of *maniera*. There are precedents for it in the Quattrocento,[97] but Mrs. Grippi's perceptive study will shed further light on this phenomenon.

Much in *maniera*, then, is like Roman relief, as if in response to Michelangelo's dictum that painting should be like relief sculpture.[98] Yet in viewing a *Battle* by Vasari (Fig. 19), one may recall what he wrote to Varchi: that painting makes a contribution of its own which an antique sculpture of fleeing soldiers, for instance, could not show: the sweat and foam, the glint of horses' coats, the hair of tails and manes, the brilliance of weapons, the reflections of figures in them, and so on.[99] To Vasari, painting's special province is pictorial detail.

But why the emphasis on detail and on its finish? The concern for pictorial detail in painting voiced by Vasari has a background in antique opinion about the advantages of painting compared to sculpture.[100] At the same time, both the detail and finish in *maniera* also suggest the influence again of antique example: in sculpture with high finish and circumstantial minutiae (Fig. 17).[101] Even behind the wish for perfection in extremities one senses rivalry with ancient sculpture; it was specifically in respect to these that Vasari compared Michelangelo and the antique.

16

An inkling of the antique-*maniera* relationship appears in eighteenth and nineteenth century comment,[102] but the twentieth century has seldom returned to the theme. Dvořák and others saw that the Raphael School had a new familiarity with the antique.[103] Antal was interested in an archaeological trend from Peruzzi to Ligorio and noted in passing that "the late antique style was congenial to Mannerism."[104] Weisbach pointed to Roman sarcophagi for the thin figures and graceful poses of Mannerism.[105] Adolf Goldschmidt, the medievalist, went nearer the heart of the matter in his article on Lambert Lombard,[106] who, with other northerners, he said, retained the sculptural character of ancient statues and relief in his work. In this style "the art-loving public .. believed it saw," as he put it, "the reflowering of the antique spirit." Recently Phyllis Bober has asserted that with the genesis of Mannerism (in which she includes and thinks particularly of early anticlassicism, as is customary) artists sought out eccentric aspects of ancient art in Hellenistic sculpture and archaistic Neo-Attic works and rediscovered Roman relief from the later second century through the third as confirmation and reinforcement of their own tendencies.[107] I shall return to this.

*   *   *

Maniera was anticipated long before Vasari's generation, but not under way in earnest until the 1530's. Except for one picture, Vasari himself apparently did not embark on it fully until about 1540.[108] Then, suddenly, he did, in the Camaldoli *Deposition* (Fig. 20) and the *Immaculate Conception* for SS. Apostoli in Florence (Fig. 2a).[109] Thereafter he never turned back. Although a prime exponent of *maniera*, he was, it seems, a slightly late comer. Two years before, for example, *maniera* was in full evidence in the *Preaching of John the Baptist* by

17

Jacopino del Conte.[110] It had been forming definitively from about 1530,[111] largely in the hands of Florentines—in Florence, Rome, Fontainebleau, and lesser centers. Bronzino was one of those principally involved in this, at the outset of the 'thirties;[112] yet about 1540, when he painted the ceiling of the Eleanora Chapel,[113] he still did not see it as the only true way. In Figure 21a, Saint Francis and Brother Leo move freely in depth. Although the scene reflects Quattrocento models,[114] it seems almost proto-Baroque, spatial and illusionistic, and light from above creates a luminous atmosphere. Exactly next to it on the ceiling is the *Saint Michael* (Fig. 21b)—flattened, angular, with marble-like limbs, flat *maniera* light, and tipped-up space.[115] In this pair is proof, if any were needed, that *maniera* is deliberate and not unwitting. Hereafter, Bronzino did not turn back either. From the later 'thirties on, in fact, *maniera* spread with the greatest speed through most of Italy and far beyond, and the long period of its sway, in various phases and guises,[116] and at greatly varying intensities,[117] began.

But *maniera* had plenty of precedents, and this was the second major factor in its development. Its conventions had begun to "germinate," to use Bellori's word, much earlier, in less extreme forms, dispersed sporadically in works of all sorts. They appeared with increasing frequency from the beginning of the second decade. One could call this, perhaps, the gathering of mid-Cinquecento *maniera*.

It would take a long time to trace the gathering of *maniera* properly. There are precedents in so-called "Neo-Gothic" painting of the Quattrocento, as exemplified, for instance, by Botticelli and Pollaiuolo, and the reasons for them include antiquizing that is related to the antiquizing behind *maniera*.[118] *Maniera* has deep roots here. There are Quattrocento instances of archaeological faithfulness to (and even some exaggeration of) antique flatness, like the medallions of the Palazzo Medici-Riccardi.[119] There is the sarcophagus-like movement of Bertoldo's battle relief.[120] Precedents occur in the work of High Renaissance artists. Despite Leonardo's fundamental contribution to classic painting, one sees them in the way he sometimes used his new vocabulary of posture and gesture, and in his light.[121] Mr. Berenson's curious essay on the ravages of his influence has some bearing here.[122] And there are precedents in those who used Leonardo's light schematically, like Albertinelli.[123]

The anticipations of *maniera* conventions in Michelangelo are inescapable, from the *Doni Madonna* and the sarcophagus-like *Battle of Cascina* on.[124] One example among the early ones is of special interest: the Lazarus that he contributed to Sebastiano's *Raising of Lazarus*.[125] The figure is flat in the *maniera* sense of flat, difficult contrapposto. It is gratifying that Mrs. Grippi has found it to have a specific antique prototype on the Phaeton sarcophagus in the Uffizi.[126] Seen from the *maniera* standpoint, the Lazarus was a ground-breaking figure and a perfect model to other painters for modernizing the antique into *maniera*. Considering also the crowding and angularity of the painting as a whole, the *Raising of Lazarus* is a landmark—if we look, that is, with the eyes of a *maniera* artist from the vantage point of mid-century. Elsewhere, too, Sebastiano was one who led toward the flattened contrapposto of *maniera*, as in his *Death of Adonis*,[127] and toward simplified contours and surfaces, beginning with his early work.

Nineteenth and twentieth century critics were sensitive to any signs of the coming "decline" in Raphael and his School. In Wölfflin's view, Raphael had temporarily lost his way in the *Parnassus*.[128] Yet we can see in its flat figures, crowding, and movement an effort to grasp another aspect of antique style,[129] prefiguring, in a mild way, the *maniera's* interest— *maniera* in a vein of *dolcezza*,[130] such as Vasari usually favored. There are forerunners of other features in many familiar works of Raphael and his School: the *Battle of Ostia*, for instance—a clear case of the antique style of Roman relief[131] upsetting High Renaissance "classic norms"[132]—and especially in the work of Giulio Romano in his own independent career.[133] But in these forerunners the conventions are not all in evidence, nor concerted in their influence, nor played upon in the bizarre modern ways of *maniera*.

Prints helped to spread antiquizing vocabulary and a taste for undifferentiating line.[134] Drawings of ancient relief, from the fifteenth century on, are a very pre-condition of *maniera*.[135]

In her book on Aspertini's drawings after the antique, Phyllis Bober suggests that with the onset of so-called early Mannerism there begins a veiled reinforcing influence from the kinds of antiquities that "express eccentric invention and a subjective, mannered deviation from rational naturalism," including Antonine and Late Antonine relief—"a secret world of antique influences" that go underground and become "progressively difficult to distinguish."[136] Pontormo's characteristic *Deposition* of the mid 'twenties in Santa Felicita,[137] with its restless movement and piled-up composition in a restricted space, bears out her view of the "veiled absorption" of Roman relief in early anticlassicism.

But the influence of relief sculpture is not so easy to distinguish in the *Deposition* as it will be later. The forced flatness of *maniera* is not here. It is not as yet a concerted application of the *maniera* conventions that defines the style. Similarly with portraits: Pontormo's young *Duke Alessandro* has none of the *maniera's* stylization, so clear in Bronzino's *Capponi*.[138] Nevertheless, as is the case with his contemporaries, in a few of Pontormo's works anticipations of *maniera* conventions appear very strongly, particularly in his Visdomini altarpiece.[139] (Meanwhile Pontormo, along with other early Tuscan anticlassicists, set precedents in painting for the eccentric inventiveness and for the sophisticated grace that would continue in the more stylized context of *maniera*. Both had been partly inspired in turn by Michelangelo.)

There is no time to follow the gathering of *maniera* in many others: Sodoma, Peruzzi, Beccafumi, Bandinelli, Polidoro, Perino, or Parmigianino, not to mention artists of less consequence. Sodoma's work at the Farnesina, for instance, is apt to be considered provincial or even medieval. But from the standpoint of a *maniera* artist it must have seemed a step toward a modern antiquizing style.[140] Peruzzi is of prime importance for *maniera* interest in antique vocabulary and, especially, eccentric antique poses, as in his *Presentation of the Virgin*. Several figures there show adaptations of antique eccentricities in pose, such as may be seen in the figure at the right on the Rospigliosi sarcophagus.[141] But as with early works of Pontormo, the essence of the style cannot be defined in terms of the set of *maniera* conventions. These are somewhat more in evidence in his print of Heracles.[142] They are still more so in Beccafumi's decorations at the Palazzo Bindi-Sergardi[143] or Bandinelli's *Martyrdom of Saint Lawrence* in the 'twenties.[144] Bandinelli's influence must have been important. In Polidoro's *all'antica* painting the chief conventions of pose and grouping are less marked,[145] but his contribution to the repertoire of *maniera* was enormous, as Vasari recognized.[146] It was somewhat the same with the early Perino.[147] Although on returning to Rome in the 'thirties he was a confirmed *maniera* painter, previously he had chiefly anticipated certain aspects of *maniera* belonging to its sweeter vein—grace, types, handling, sometimes also compositional schemes. So had Parmigianino,[148] building partly on Correggio and Raphael; and his ideal facial types undoubtedly were continued by Salviati, Vasari, and others. But then, in his work of the later 'twenties and around 1530, the chief conventions of *maniera* began to coalesce.[149]

Indeed, it was around 1530 that the gathering of *maniera* was stepped up, even though, as Hartt has pointed out, a certain restraint can be discerned at this moment, compared to the 1520's.[150] There were strong precedents for *maniera* in

Rosso before 1530, especially in his *Moses and the Daughters of Jethro*;[151] now, however, in the upper corners of the *Transfiguration*, he introduced the new flat figures with two twists of direction. [152] In 1531, inspired partly by Rosso's picture, Bronzino at Pesaro transformed a reclining pose of Sebastiano del Piombo's into something like *maniera* (Fig. 22)[153] and designed a female allegorical figure, on the basis particularly of the antique and Dürer, that really embodies *maniera* ideals of pose and contour as well as elegance (Fig. 23). On his return to Florence shortly afterward, his importance for the development of *maniera* was no doubt very considerable.[154]

The chief impetus, however, must have come at this moment from Michelangelo. As a recent study by Wilde indicates,[155] he achieved about 1530 a special clarity and purity in surface arrangement under the guidance of antique relief. And he now employed what were to be some of the dominant *maniera* conventions in a more concerted way than before. The drawings of the *Fall of Phaeton* and the *Dream* represent this. The main figure of the *Dream* goes back to the Lazarus, and the prototypes for both it and the *Phaeton* are found on the same sarcophagus.[156] From various instances, we know how this style of Michelangelo's interested some of the masters who now embarked on *maniera*.[157]

In the course of the 1530's the conventions became rooted and intensified, to work in concert and dominate the main stream of painting. The more they were intensified, the more old fundamentals for posing figures were transformed into something different. Poses were derived from earlier painting and the antique. Doubtless not without some influence from more general developments in taste[158] and from growing sophistication, they were given more elegance,[159] more refinement, more brawn, more directions,[160] more dislocation, more flatness-plus-foreshortening—that is, more grace, difficulty, novelty, and curiousness in the framework of the conventions

(Fig. 2a, b). It is as if painters raised in familiarity with the antique, conversant with all Cinquecento painting in Central Italy, and conditioned by the experimentation of the 'twenties, had said: "The antique and inventiveness interest all of us. Let our painting stress both. Let us work with the antique and precedents in Cinquecento painting, Michelangelo above all, but also Raphael and the others,[161] and go as much farther as we possibly can." And they now set out with a certain optimism, I think, to judge from the freshness of their work in the 'thirties[162] and early 'forties.

*　*　*

For one must be aware of *maniera's* possibilities and virtues. Vasari says with respect specifically to painting that within the *regola* there must be *licenzia*: within the rule, there must be license.[163] *Regola* in architecture, Vasari had just said, means observing the measures and plans of antique buildings in modern ones. He does not redefine it for painting. With this in mind, I am tempted to think *regola* in painting and drawing may be read as "the antique-derived rules," or conventions, of *maniera*.[164] True or not, if we choose, temporarily, to read it this way, Vasari's formula conveys a *maniera* fundamental: within its set of antique-derived conventions, promoting ideal uniformity, there must be license—license, variation, surprise, within the *maniera* rule.[165] The style can be appreciated only if the observer sees both the set of conventions and the license within them. The conventions constituted a scale on which to play. But since, after the Cinquecento, the ear for this scale was largely lost, it is not always easy to appreciate what is played on it.

It is in drawings especially that modern eyes, attuned to the sketch more than to the finished *maniera* painting, can see how the sensitive artist found possibilities in *maniera* for in-

23

vention, variation, self-expression, and a diversity of modes. Vasari speaks of such diversity,[166] and his own drawings reflect it. In Figure 24, a finished study, he is hard, clear, detailed; in Figure 25, his line is fluent and free; in Figure 26, working in wash alone, he is interested in relief and indentation, light and dark. As a draftsman he brings forth endless configurations, chiefly obeying *maniera* rule, but nonetheless various, as a sympathetic, veteran eye immediately sees. His is not variety that depends primarily on nature's variety, desired by Dolce.[167] It is more a matter of diverse forms of writing and of fresh inventions and combinations, tumbling from the pen.[168] So also with Naldini, Vasari's follower, in two drawings surprisingly different from each other, yet both made for accepted works (Figs. 27, 28).[169] *Maniera* had found an emancipating power in its helpmate *pratica*, in the readiness of the practised hand,[170] freed of the need to consult nature and properly prepared to enjoy its own facility. In drawings, the result is a little like "action painting," supported, however, by the rigor of the style's principles.[171]

There can be comparable diversity also in *maniera* painting, despite its finish. But in black and white reproductions diversity is partly suppressed, because color so often plays a role in it. Color in *maniera* still needs to be properly valued and explored. Standing, for example, in the Cappella Salviati of San Marco before the altarpieces of Poppi (Fig. 8), Naldini, and Allori (Fig. 4), one sees something of the variety of treatment possible in even the purest of *maniera* painting. And here also one can imagine how sparse and how bare of invention works like that by Fra Bartolommeo, across the church, must have seemed to mid-Cinquecento taste.

Maniera, with its flattened figures, is in its element as decorative enrichment, encrusting walls, tapestries, and minor objects.[172] At the same time we are learning not to ignore even the small parts of a large decoration when a master of *maniera* is involved. Salviati's *Birth of the Virgin* in San Mar-

24

cello (Fig. 29) shows what charm inventiveness with figures, divisions of space for surprise,[173] and sensitive light can have in good hands. It is among the pleasures to be had from *maniera* to see a perceptive, adventuresome artist like Salviati introduce novelty within the framework of the conventions and also breathe back some of the sensuous feeling of organic life into the conventionalized forms without spoiling the artificial world.[174]

Some could use the idiom with high seriousness and emotion—Pontormo, for example, who adopted it like everyone else for his later work, but with haunting effect (Fig. 30), or El Greco (Fig. 31), who took advantage of its conventions, above all the flat light, for his own extraordinary purposes.[175]

And in general it can be said of *maniera* that, however prone to extravagance, it achieved, with its rigorous conventions, with its reluctance to concede to flesh-and-blood reality, a formality and distance. These were weakened in the anti-mannerist reform. One can well argue that this meant a loss as well as a gain.

The *maniera* painters themselves were clearly as concerned with the vocabulary of pose and gesture as with any other aspect of their art—often more so. It should itself be a study for the historian and critic,[176] for in order to appreciate fully what an individual painter was doing, one must be well acquainted with the vocabulary.

It is worth recalling, finally, that once released from the conventions, *maniera's* copiousness of twisting figures was fundamental for future developments in the Baroque.[177]

*   *   *

But there were pitfalls in *maniera*, and their effects are known to all. First, the close relation to antique relief. For the stone has left its stamp, as Rubens wrote in his warning

25

on the use of sculptural models by painters.[178] He was writing
for those who think to form their style from sculpture, much
of it bad. Among the results, he cited crudeness,[179] stony
modeling and color, abrupt shadows, and bright, even light
on the surfaces. One can add: dehumanization, loss of
vitality and sensuous plastic power, the acceptance of slack
structure, bland surfaces, de-individualization, monotony,
and the relief-inspired disruption of painterly coherence.[180]
The hazard was not primarily helpless academic decay, but
preference for the qualities of antique sculpture.[181] Also, in
maniera's desire for a uniform ideal lay the possibility of
monotony and routine; in the desire for license, difficulty,
and abundant invention lay the likelihood of straining and
over-elaboration.[182] The ideal of accelerated production
risked shallowness.[183] *Maniera* conventions, nearly irresistible
and easily assimilated, could both submerge individuality[184]
and bring a degree of success within reach of the mediocre.[185]
Maniera's leveling power comes from them.[186]

Ever since the Cinquecento itself, the resulting loss of
quality in *maniera* painting has been decried. But loss of
quality is not what defines *maniera*. It went with much of it
because of *maniera's* nature.

*   *

      *

Malvasia judged *maniera* a departure, not imitation.[187] At
the least it is something quite distinct. Imitation of one
painter's style or one school does not describe it. One could
have the conventions with or without Michelangelo's muscular types, with or without Raphael's *dolcezza*.[188] But *maniera*
did involve a general acceptance of conventions growing in
various stylistic contexts,[189] largely deriving, ultimately, from
antique relief and reinforced by it again and again through
continual study. Once accepted, they constituted a scheme

26

connected with the idealizing and "modernly" antiquizing aims of painting, a *schema* in the minds, eyes, and hands of all, or nearly all—to the neglect of the new Renaissance approach to nature.[190] As the *maniera* artist looked back, the classic solution probably seemed a short-lived interlude in the evolution of the modern style[191] (which Vasari traced for us) and the precedents for this style among High Renaissance painters sufficient to keep him feeling at one with them—not in opposition.[192]

*   *   *

If this is a justified view of what was historically called *maniera*, there remains the question: what relation do modern concepts of Mannerism bear to it that have developed from it since?

Apart from the principal modern concept, there is, first, an assortment of others in which Mannerism is seen as a more or less general, recurring phenomenon. Of these, Mannerism as the domination of formulae,[193] Mannerism as dependence on earlier achievements,[194] Mannerism as elaboration (often for unexpected effects) in which form is not naturally suited to the subject,[195] Mannerism as intensification and stiffening, leading, nevertheless, to Baroque movement,[196] Mannerism as artificiality and affectation,[197] and Mannerism as refinement[198]—all fit more or less. But each concerns only an aspect, and none by itself does it justice.[199] Moreover, *maniera* emerges as a special instance of each, one that cannot be separated from the circumstances of art and art theory at its own moment.

Of concepts concerned specifically with Cinquecento painting, the nineteenth century's view of Mannerism as adherence to a manner full of unjustified, habitual peculiarities may fit *maniera* judged in relation to reality, but fits much less well judged in relation to *maniera's* antiquizing and

27

idealizing purposes. More recent concepts of sixteenth century Mannerism in which the emphasis is on grace, elegance, or refinement[200] pertain to important aspects of the ideal for the human figure. The *maniera* artist himself was outspoken about them; and we know from Weise that the word *maniera* had an old association with style in deportment, aiming at elegance. Yet the main emphasis, in definitions of this kind, is not on the central phenomenon of modern antiquizing, idealizing uniformity, to which Dolce and Vasari point, but on attributes of it.[201]

The present-day conception of Mannerism, as primarily a deliberate deviation from nature and the classic norm of the High Renaissance, moves farther away. It shifts the focus to license, and not to license within the conventions (*nella regola una licenzia*, as I would read it), but to license in relation to nature and to the High Renaissance, following the Seicento's lead. This view is not primarily directed at painting showing *maniera* in Dolce's sense,[202] but at an earlier stage in painting.

Yet on it is built the salient concept of the present time: Mannerism as a subjective art expressing a spiritual situation through anticlassic forms, deformation, and abstraction. Not only is Mannerism in this sense now considered valid for the Cinquecento, but it begins to be applied as the name for a subjective, surrealistic, anticlassic phenomenon that critics see recurring in European art. It is becoming the name for the manifestation of a rebellious, expressionistic "constant of the European spirit."[203] This is a concept that has still less to do with the fundamentals of *maniera*—even though, put less drastically, it bears a relation to what was done with the *maniera* idiom by artists like Pontormo in his late work, or by El Greco.

*   *   *

28

These last concepts of deviation and expressionism are intimately linked to modern ideas about the anticlassic developments of the 1520's and somewhat before, particularly in Tuscan painting—developments represented by the early Pontormo, for one. The relation of these developments to *maniera* is difficult to define because of the lack of agreement about what they were in themselves.

I tend to subscribe to Ernst Gombrich's view that the anticlassic style of the 'twenties was connected with the desire to experiment and contribute something new rather than with a spiritual crisis.[204] It was, it seems to me, experiment with other possibilities then claiming attention more than out-and-out revolt. The sources of impetus and inspiration were Michelangelo, antique, "Neo-Gothic," German, whatever could help, the first two especially; and neither of these was an unorthodox model.[205] As for the antique, the influence of Roman relief was much in evidence. I should say, not merely that it reinforced the anticlassic developments of the early Cinquecento, but that it was probably, in the last analysis, their original fountainhead.[206] Even behind "expressionism," such as Rosso's, may well be antique faces, like one on a sarcophagus in the Villa Borghese (Fig. 32).[207]

But if the early post-classic experiments and *maniera* have Roman relief and Michelangelo as sources in common, the results are not for the most part the same. We cannot adequately define both by what defines *maniera*.

I assume we shall persist in calling the post-classic innovations of the second and third decades Mannerism because we have done so for forty years. But, strictly speaking, we should consider as proper early Mannerism, I think, only those productions of the earlier painting that clearly anticipate the fundamentals of *maniera*.[208] By this criterion, Pontormo's Visdomini altarpiece would qualify rather well, his *Christ before Pilate* (Fig. 1) much less,[209] his lunette at Poggio a Caiano (Fig. 33) scarcely at all—however sensitive, refined, abstract, private, irrational, or eccentrically expressive. Even after the 1530's a similar criterion applies. *Maniera* is not equally in evidence in all works, even by the same master. The less so, the less appropriate the term Mannerism seems to be.[210]

But what about the need of a term for the whole span from the beginning of post-classic painting to the Carracci and Caravaggio? Does not the early development, from classic painting to post-classic innovation, stand out as a more crucial departure than the development from the latter to *maniera?* Should not this entire span, therefore, be under one name? I should say the more non-committal the name the better at this juncture, so that we can grasp the range and intricacies of Cinquecento painting as clearly as possible, unswayed by a term. Our view of the period 1515/20 to 1585/90 ought not to be subject to any distortion by the potent implications attached to Mannerism since the Seicento.[211] Voss and a few others have thought that "Late Renaissance" served the purpose for painting in this period.[212] Judged by the extent of the rebirth of antiquity in painting, this does not seem a misnomer.

If we do continue to include all the earlier post-classic painting under Mannerism and if we do keep the name as a synonym for anticlassic (or unclassic) expressionism, which is now found to be such an important general phenomenon in art,[213] the main thing is to understand what we are doing, what the liberties are that we agree to take with the old use of *maniera*. This may help diminish the danger of viewing Cinquecento painting, as a whole and in detail, in a way that is partial in any sense. And the same would apply, I should think, to transferring the term Mannerism to other arts—to architecture, for example, if we continue to find it useful.[214]

Notes

1. E. H. Gombrich, "The Historiographic Background," *Acts of the XXth International Congress of Art Historians, Studies of Western Art*, Princeton University Press, forthcoming, volume II. This was Gombrich's introduction to the session on "Recent Concepts of Mannerism," of which he was chairman, and was sent to the speakers in advance.

2. See the convenient (though incomplete) bibliography on Mannerism in the catalogue of the exhibition at Naples, July-October, 1952: *Fontainebleau e la maniera italiana*, Florence, 1952, pp. 71 ff.

3. Walter Friedlaender, "Die Entstehung des antiklassischen Stiles in der italienischen Malerei um 1520," *Repertorium für Kunstwissenschaft*, XLVI, 1925, pp. 49 ff., translated and republished in Walter Friedlaender, *Mannerism and Anti-mannerism in Italian Painting*, New York, 1957, pp. 3 ff.

4. Mario Salmi, "La mostra del cinquecento toscano," *Nuova antologia*, LXXV, no. 410, July-August, 1940, pp. 75–83; Paola Barocchi, *Il Rosso Fiorentino*, Rome, 1950, pp. 231–240; C. Gamba, *Contributo alla conoscenza del Pontormo*, Florence, 1956, pp. 5–7. E. Baldwin Smith and Leo Steinberg expressed similar doubts to me which spurred my interest. See also the essay by Luisa Becherucci cited in footnote 23 below.

5. For the distinction between "classic" and "classical" adhered to in this paper (except in quoting the now common term "the anti-classical style," which is the customary translation of Friedlaender's *der antiklassische Stil*), see Denis Mahon, *Studies in Seicento Art and Theory*, London, 1947, pp. 11–12 and H. Wölfflin, *Principles of Art History*, New York, 1932, p. 15, translator's note: namely, "classic" referring, like Wölfflin's *klassisch*, to the art of the High Renaissance and also implying "a special mode of creation of which that art is an instance," and "classical" denoting a relation to antiquity.

The term *antiklassisch* has also been used with respect to developments in German painting after Dürer: see H. Wescher-Kauert, "Das Ende der altdeutschen Malerei und die antiklassische Strömung," *Cicerone*, XVI, 1924, pp. 996 ff.

6. Gio. Pietro Bellori, *Le vite de' pittori, scultori et architetti moderni*, Rome, 1672, pp. 19–20. See also the comparable statements by G. B. Agucchi in Mahon, *Studies in Seicento Art and Theory*, p. 247; C. C. Malvasia, *Felsina pittrice*, Bologna, 1678, I, p. 358; F. Baldinucci, *Notizie dei professori del disegno da Cimabue in qua*, Florence, 1767–76, XII, p. 69 (in the life of Guido Reni); and G. B. Passeri, *Delle vite de' pittori scultori et architetti* in J. Hess, *Die Künstlerbiographien von Giovanni Battista Passeri*, Leipzig and Vienna, 1934, pp. 6 and 12.

According to Bellori, painting had reached a height with Raphael. But after Raphael (Bellori does not make clear exactly when) there was suddenly a decline. "Artists," he says, "abandoning the study of nature, corrupted art with *la maniera* or if you prefer fantastic idea based on *pratica* and not on the imitation [of nature]." He goes on: "This vice, destroyer of painting, began to germinate in masters of honored reputation and became rooted in the schools that then followed. Wherefore, it is incredible how much they degenerated not only in comparison with Raphael but with the others who initiated *la maniera*. Florence, which prided itself on being the mother of painting, and the whole region of Tuscany, which was illustrious by reason of its painters, already were silent . . . and the others of the School of Rome, no longer raising their eyes to look at the abundance of examples, antique and modern, had forgotten every praiseworthy advantage [to be obtained from them]."

The Malvasia passage reads: "[Ludovico Carracci] was born in 1555, precisely in the time when the followers and pupils of the schools mentioned above dared to depart from [the example of] the heads of those schools, in fact from their own masters, through what lazy ignorance, or vain rashness, I do not know. Seeking another mode and a different way of doing things they became addicted to weak, not to say incorrect, *disegno*, to feeble washed-out color, in short to a certain *maniera* far from verisimilitude and from the truth, totally chimerical and ideal, although at the same time copious and perhaps also too resolute. These were Salviati, the Zuccari, Vasari,

Andrea Vicentino, Tomaso Laureti, and of our [Bolognese painters] Samacchini, Sabbattini, Calvaert, the Procaccini, and the like. Abandoning the imitation of antique statues, not to mention a good imitation of nature, they based themselves wholly on their imagination and applied themselves to a certain way of working that was quick and completely *manieroso*. Such was also Prospero Fontana, the first director and master of our Ludovico ..."

7. See footnote 26 below.

8. Nineteenth century formulations consistently show the basic concept outlined here. They vary—but not greatly—in the related aspects that they stress. A list of these would include: repetition of formulae and eccentricities based largely on the imitated style, sameness from work to work and artist to artist, neglect of nature (except in prosaic details); also arbitrariness, affectation, capricious imaginativeness, and art for art's sake instead of a higher purpose; hence emptiness coupled with mere decorativeness, extravagant display in which form and object are not sufficiently merged, over-accentuation of grace and refinement, overemphasis on Michelangelesque muscular nudes multiplied in exaggerated, meaningless poses; at the same time crowding, lack of space, confusion, incorrect drawing, careless speed, hardness, lifelessness, and feeble color.

For a sampling of nineteenth century opinion on Mannerism in the Cinquecento, see: Luigi Lanzi, *Storia pittorica dell'Italia*, Bassano, 1795–96, I, pp. 168 ff., 206 ff., 431 ff., 598 ff. and also pp. 417–418, 425; II, part ii, pp. 38–39, 47 ff.; J. D. Fiorillo, *Geschichte der Mahlerei*, Göttingen, 1798, I, especially pp. 123 ff., 139–142, 151 to 152, 155, 338, 345, 358–359, 368, and 377 ff. (Fiorillo expresses well the opinion that remained more or less standard for the nineteenth century); C. F. von Rumohr, *Italienische Forschungen*, Berlin and Stettin, 1827–1831, I, pp. 35 ff., II, pp. 399 ff. and especially 411 ff.; Franz Kugler, *Handbuch der Geschichte der Malerei seit Constantin dem Grossen*, 3rd edition, revised by H. v. Blomberg, Leipzig, 1867, II, pp. 342 ff. and also p. 252; J. Burckhardt, *Der Cicerone*, Basel, 1855, pp. 994 ff.; P. Selvatico, *Storico estetico—Critica delle arti del disegno*, Venice, 1852/1856, II, pp. 737 ff.; H. Grimm, *Neue Essays über Kunst und Literatur*, Berlin, 1865, pp. 250 ff.; John Addington Symonds, *Renaissance in Italy, The Fine Arts*, London, 1906 (original ed. 1876), pp. 359 ff.; G. Ebe, *Die Spätrenaissance*, Berlin, 1886, pp. 93 ff., 185 ff.; Eugène Müntz, *Histoire de l'art pendant la renaissance*, III, *Italie, la fin de la renaissance*, Paris, 1895, pp. 4, 91 ff., 170, 217; Romain Rolland, *De la décadence de la peinture italienne au XVIe siècle*, Albin Michel, Paris, 1957, *passim* (the original French text of a thesis in Latin of 1895, of which a résumé was published in *La revue de Paris*, January, 1896, pp. 168–202); August Schmarsow, *Barock und Rokoko*, Leipzig, 1897, pp. 176 ff.; J. Strzygowski, *Das Werden des Barockstils bei Raphael und Correggio*, Strasbourg, 1898, pp. 80 ff.; H. Wölfflin, *Classic Art*, London, 1952, (original edition 1899), pp. 202–204; A. Riegl, *Die Entstehung der Barockkunst in Rom. Akademische Vorlesungen*, Vienna, 1908 (dating from about 1900), pp. 142 ff.; F. X. Kraus, *Geschichte der christlichen Kunst*, II, part 2 (continued and published by Joseph Sauer), Freiburg im Breisgau, 1908, pp. 782 ff.

While the whole oeuvre of Michelangelo was thought conducive to peculiarities in the work of imitators, the *Last Judgment* and the sculptures of the Medici Chapel loomed largest in this respect. Uncomprehending imitation of these was the main factor in the decline. (Symonds was exceptional, *op. cit.*, p. 361, in referring to "Michelangelo's mighty mannerism." Schmarsow, *op. cit.*, pp. 56 and 176, added an opposite twist when he suggested that the Mannerists failed to comprehend the baroque implications of the *Last Judgment* and Medici tombs and, hence, to play a proper part in the history of the baroque style.)

Michelangelo imitation was thought the one most important cause of Mannerism in Florence. Mannerism in Rome was often traced to imitation of Michelangelo, but not always or exclusively. The superficial imitation of Raphael, of Raphael in his more Michelangelesque aspects, and sometimes of antique sculpture also opened the way to it. In the opinion of some, imitation of antique sculpture without proper understanding was conducive to decline because it could bring on stiffness, hardness, and isolation of figures from each other. (See, for example: Lanzi, *op. cit.*, I, pp. 417–418; Fiorillo, *op. cit.*, I, pp. 123 ff.; Müntz, *op. cit.*, III, pp. 125–126; Rolland, *op. cit.*, pp. 53 ff.; also Strzygowski, *op. cit.*, pp. 50 ff., 83; Marcel Raymond, *De Michelange à Tiepolo*, Paris, 1912, pp. 6 ff.) Fiorillo and Rolland emphasize particularly that the bad influence of antiquity begins to be evident with Giulio Romano, preparing the way for Mannerism, or decline.

For views on anticipations of Mannerism before the 1530's among Raphael's immediate followers (especially Giulio Romano)—who were not, however, called Mannerists—and sometimes even in works of Raphael himself, see Fiorillo, *op. cit.*, I, p. 132; Kugler, *op. cit.*, II, pp. 136, 233, 258 ff. and pp. 345 ff.; J. D. Passavant, *Rafael von Urbino und sein Vater Giovanni Santi*, Leipzig, 1839–1858, I, pp. 370 ff.; Burckhardt, *op. cit.*, I, pp. 937 ff. and 994 ff.; H. Grimm, "Raphael's Ruhm" in *Das Leben Raphaels*, 2nd ed., Berlin, 1886, p. 13; Rolland, *op. cit.*, pp. 51 ff. and pp. 42–43 on Raphael's *Entombment;* Strzygowski, *op. cit.*, p. 83. There was some thought that the decline itself had overtaken the late works of Giulio and Perino del Vaga: the decorations in the Sala di Troia by the former (Kugler, *op. cit.*, II, p. 255) and Perino's painting after his return to Rome in the late 'thirties (and even before at Genoa: Selvatico, *op. cit.*, II, pp. 737 ff.).

In the school of Parma, the sweetness of Correggio was considered to have been falsely understood by his followers, including Parmigianino, but again, it was not customary to label Parmigianino a Mannerist. See, for example, Lanzi, *op. cit.*, II, i, p. 322; Kugler, *op. cit.*, II, pp. 292 ff., 345 ff.; Burckhardt, *op. cit.*, p. 959; Ebe, *op. cit.*, p. 185. Rolland, *op. cit.*, pp. 68 ff. speaks, however, of the mannerism of Correggio and of Parmigianino as heir to it.

Anticipations of Mannerism were sometimes seen in the early work of Rosso, but less in that of Pontormo. Some thought the decline itself affected the later work of Pontormo, Beccafumi, and Parmigianino as well, yet none of the four was classed as a Mannerist. See for example: Fiorillo, *op. cit.*, pp. 336, 388 ff.; Kugler, *op. cit.*, II, pp. 166, 167, 292, 293; Burckhardt, *op. cit.*, pp. 888–889, 948, 959, 994; Ebe, *op. cit.*, p. 185; Rolland, *op. cit.*, p. 80 for Parmigianino, pp. 39 and 86 for Rosso; Symonds, *op. cit.*, p. 367 for Beccafumi. Lanzi, *op. cit.*, I, p. 148 considered, however, that Pontormo entered a fourth phase with the *Deluge* at San Lorenzo, showing the same imitation of Michelangelo and the anatomical style that was popular then in Florence.

While critics had little difficulty in agreeing as to who were the sixteenth century Mannerists proper and in distinguishing them from those who merely anticipated Mannerism, some used the term

Mannerism for seventeenth and eighteenth century painting, too, thinking to see abuses there similar to those they found in the Cinquecento and believing the reform at the end of the Cinquecento not entirely successful. See, for example, Lanzi, *op. cit.*, II, i, pp. 148 ff.; Rumohr, *op. cit.*, pp. 41 ff.; and Selvatico, *op. cit.*, II, p. 740. This view, too, goes back to the seventeenth century, when it is expressed by R. Fréart de Chambray, *Idée de la perfection de la peinture*, Le Mans, 1662, p. 120. Romain Rolland, *op. cit.*, p. 27, was in a sense continuing it when he maintained that the Carracci only succeeded in eliminating one element of the decadence, the influence of Michelangelo. A parallel use of "mannerist" and "mannerism" for the Baroque of the seventeenth and eighteenth centuries occurs occasionally also with respect to architecture (cf. Marco Treves, "*Maniera*, the History of the Word," *Marsyas*, I, 1941, p. 80).

A short survey of opinion relating to Mannerism from the sixteenth to the twentieth century is given by G. Briganti, *Il manierismo e Pellegrino Tibaldi*, Rome, 1945, pp. 39–49.

9. Müntz, *op. cit.*, III, p. 91. A similar view had been expressed about the decline in sixteenth century painting by Bellori, and Vasari had remarked on the growth and decay of art in biological terms. Müntz was puzzled by the vitality in science and music contemporary with the degeneration of painting, and glimpsed some vitality even in painting itself (III, p. 217).

Fiorillo, *op. cit.*, I, pp. 152 ff., compared the situation to that of an individual painter at any period: even though he might have a creative, original style formed, as it should be, on nature and the study of a variety of artists rather than one, he was likely, once his work had gained approval, to become mannered from repeating and exaggerating himself.

10. In explaining in this way the development of error about a decade after Raphael, Rumohr began characteristically to move in the direction of modern observations: the laziness and vanity of painters gave rise to their belief that "it is given to the artist to develop forms out of himself which surpass the natural in significance and beauty," whence their "wanton invention and arbitrary dexterity." See Rumohr, *op. cit.*, I, p. 35, also II, p. 413.

11. These reasons partly reflect sixteenth century views about the factors that brought a falling off of quality in painting, of which the Cinquecento itself became increasingly conscious. See, for example, Paolo Pino, *Dialogo di pittura*, Venice, 1548, republished in Paola Barocchi, *Trattati d'arte del cinquecento fra manierismo e controriforma*, Bari, 1960–61, I, p. 108; Ludovico Dolce, *Dialogo della pittura, intitolato l'Aretino*, Venice, 1557, in Barocchi, *op. cit.*, I, p. 206; and G. B. Armenini, *De' veri precetti della pittura*, Ravenna, 1587, pp. 9 ff. Both artists and patrons were blamed.

12. See especially Müntz, *op. cit.*, III, pp. 99 ff., and Romain Rolland, *op. cit.*, p. 27 and pp. 31 ff.

13. Riegl, *op. cit.*, p. 154.
As a rule the nineteenth century saw Mannerism as the degeneration of an old style. There are only small inklings of anything more positive. Burckhardt, *op. cit.*, p. 998, implied that it had a definite aim when he called it a false "Pompstil" (a name possibly derived from Gilio) and noted that artists were capable of very good work where the "Pompstil" left off, as in portraits. See also Lanzi, *op. cit.*, II, ii, p. 53. Kugler almost recognized a change in the stylistic basis of painting. He wrote (*op. cit.*, II, p. 293) of "a false direction working on artists from without rather than inability" and (p. 343) found that artists who years earlier would have done great things were now no longer supported by the "Fluidum" of measure and beauty that previously had enabled even mediocre painters to achieve great creations. Riegl did not think the Mannerists ground-breaking, but various contemporary phenomena persuaded him they belonged to a new period. Müntz (*op. cit.*, III, p. 4) excluded them from the Renaissance, but only on the grounds that they lacked originality.

14. As frequently observed. See, for instance, H. Hoffmann, *Hochrenaissance, Manierisimus, Frühbarock, die italienische Kunst des 16. Jahrhunderts*, Zurich-Leipzig, 1938, p. 6.

15. Cf. Max Dvořák, "Über Greco und den Manierismus," *Kunstgeschichte als Geistesgeschichte*, Munich, 1928, (originally delivered in 1920), pp. 275–276 (the passage is cited by Gombrich in "Recent

Concepts of Mannerism, the Historiographic Background," *op. cit.*). For an English translation by John Coolidge, see *Magazine of Art*, XLVI, No. 1, 1953, p. 23.

16. Cf. footnote 6. See also Giustiniani's definition (without disapproval) of "dipignere di maniera" as the mode in which "the painter, with long *pratica* in *disegno* and coloring, of his own fancy and without any model paints what he has in his fancy" (in Giovanni Bottari and S. Ticozzi, *Raccolta di lettere sulla pittura, scultura, ed architettura*, Milan, 1822, VI, p. 125). See also Baldinucci, *Notizie dei professori*, XV, p. 58.

17. The first to do this clearly, I think, was Bernard Berenson in *The Drawings of the Florentine Painters*, New York, 1903, I, part 2, pp. 303–305: "No doubt these [Pontormo, Rosso, Parmigianino, and Cellini] are the names of mannerists, of people who took the first strides downward and away from the one and only ideal" out of a desire for novelty, or the wish to assert individuality, or from "the waywardness of their temperament." But theirs was not a direct vision. They played with beauty, isolating and stressing some aspect of their predecessors' achievements, for the sake of decoration, distinction, elegance, and grace. It is interesting, however, that "winsome waywardness" is included as part of the attraction of these artists, foreshadowing subsequent views, and that Berenson classifies them with the phrase "the first gifted mannerists," to distinguish them from those to come.

18. Mannerism was also found now to be in early evidence elsewhere, especially in Rome among Raphael's assistants, even in some of Raphael's own late work, and in the work of Peruzzi. See, for example, Friedlaender, *Mannerism and Anti-mannerism*, p. 19 and Pevsner in N. Pevsner and O. Grautoff, *Die Barockmalerei in den romanischen Ländern*, Potsdam, 1928, pp. 14 ff. or more recently F. Antal, "Observations on Girolamo da Carpi," *Art Bulletin*, XXX, 1948, p. 85, note 25 and A. M. Brizio, "Lorenzo Lotto e i primi avii del manierismo in Roma," *XVIIIth International Congress of the History of Art*, Venice, 1955, pp. 262–265.

19. It was almost as if some law in art history saw to the transformation of derogatory terms: see L. Fröhlich-Bum, *Parmigianino und der Manierismus*, Vienna, 1921, p. 120.

20. For the stress on the spiritual basis of Mannerism, see especially Dvořák, *op. cit.*, pp. 261 ff. (Coolidge translation, *op. cit.*, pp. 5 ff.). For Dvořák's full treatment of Italian Mannerism, see Max Dvořák, *Geschichte der italienischen Kunst im Zeitalter der Renaissance,* Munich, 1927–1929, II, pp. 118–199. (The Florentine developments do not receive the main emphasis: see pp. 164 ff.).

For lists and interpretations of twentieth century contributions concerning Mannerism, see G. N. Fasola, "Storiografia del manierismo," *Scritti di storia dell' arte in onore di Lionello Venturi,* Rome, 1956, I, pp. 429 ff.; also G. Briganti, *Il manierismo e Pellegrino Tibaldi,* pp. 45 ff.; E. Battisti, "Lo spirito del manierismo," *Letteratura,* IV, nos. 21–22, May-August, 1956, pp. 3–10; and *idem, Rinascimento e barocco,* Turin, 1960, the essay "Sfortune del manierismo," pp. 216–237 (called to my attention by Naomi Miller shortly before this paper went to press). They accept, more or less, the modern view that has resulted, although Italian criticism tends to emphasize the intellectual play and subtle stylistic aspects of Mannerism, beginning with R. Longhi, *Precisioni nelle gallerie italiane,* I, *R. Galleria Borghese,* Rome, 1928, pp. 13–14.

For an earlier review of twentieth century opinion, see Fröhlich-Bum, *op. cit.*, pp. 121–123. For the most recent review of concepts of Mannerism, published just before this manuscript went to press, see *Manierismo, barocco, rococò: concetti e termini,* Convegno internazionale, Roma, 21–24 Aprile 1960, relazioni e discussioni, Accademia Nazionale dei Lincei, Quaderno n. 52, Rome, 1962, pp. 19–20, 27–38, and *passim* in pp. 57–79.

How far the principal modern concept of Mannerism has gone can be found in Arnold Hauser, *The Social History of Art,* London, 1951, I, pp. 353 ff.; Wylie Sypher, *Four Stages of Renaissance Style,* Garden City, 1955, pp. 99 ff.; and G. R. Hocke, *Die Welt als Labyrinth,* Hamburg, 1957, especially pp. 225–226.

21. Werner Weisbach, "Zum Problem des Manierismus," *Studien zur deutschen Kunstgeschichte,* Strasbourg, 1934, p. 15.

Weisbach's contributions to the study of Mannerism are relatively neglected and deserve re-reading. If taken solely as an introduction to mature Mannerism (see the next paragraph), the observations in his "Der Manierismus," *Zeitschrift für bildende Kunst,* N. F. XXX, 1919, pp. 161 ff. are good—even though he did not come to grips with its formal principles and made no distinction between the works of Pontormo's generation in the 1520's and later Mannerism, not even the usual one based on the degree of decadence. He would not see the more "expressive" aspect of the former and declared all Cinquecento Mannerism a "no-style." Cf. also his *Manierismus in mittelalterlicher Kunst*, Basel, 1942, pp. 8 ff. and *Stilbegriffe und Stilphänomene*, Vienna, 1957, pp. 71 ff.

22. For later Mannerism as the unwitting deterioration of early Mannerism, see for example Walter Friedlaender, "Der antimanieristische Stil um 1590 und sein Verhältnis zum Übersinnlichen," *Vorträge der Bibliothek Warburg*, 1928/1929, pp. 214 ff., translated in Friedlaender, *Mannerism and Antimannerism*, pp. 48 ff.; or Briganti, *op. cit.*, p. 54. However, something of the nineteenth century distinction between painting in the 'thirties and 'forties and what had gone before was retained by others: as in the case of Dvořák, who distinguished a new wave of Mannerism stemming from Michelangelo's *Last Judgment*, even calling it a new style (see his *Geschichte der italienischen Kunst*, II, pp. 118–119, 128).

23. See footnote 4 above.
   Recently Luisa Becherucci has expressed a view that recalls some held by nineteenth century critics, namely, that Mannerism is the weakening of Raphael's style, Raphael's language "spoken by weak voices," not a development from the early Florentine anticlassicism of Pontormo and Rosso, which she no longer calls Mannerism and believes enjoyed little diffusion: see L. Becherucci, "Momenti dell'arte fiorentina nel cinquecento," in Libera cattedra di storia della civiltà fiorentina (Unione fiorentina), *Il cinquecento*, Florence, Sansoni, 1955, pp. 161 ff. and especially p. 173 (I owe my acquaintance with this essay to Sydney Freedberg).

24. See Friedlaender, *Mannerism and Anti-mannerism*, p. 50 and C. H. Smyth, "The Earliest Works of Bronzino," *Art Bulletin*, XXXI, 1949, p. 204. Cf. also the negative Mannerism and positive Mannerism of R. Sobotta, *Michelangelo und der Barockstil*, Berlin, 1933, p. 68.

25. For misgivings of this kind, see J. Q. van Regteren Altena, "Two Sixteenth-Century Exhibitions in Holland," *Burlington Magazine*,

XCVII, 1955, pp. 315–316; Donato Sanminiatelli, "The Beginnings of Domenico Beccafumi," *Burlington Magazine*, XCIX, 1957, p. 401; Riccardo Scrivano, *Il manierismo nella letteratura del cinquecento*, Padua, 1959, pp. 129 ff.; and Jean Rouchette, *La renaissance que nous a léguée Vasari*, Paris, 1959, p. 97.

26. Seventeenth century writers (see footnote 6) did not trace the decline in sixteenth century painting to exclusive, uncomprehending imitation of one previous style or to imitation of previous masters at all, as already observed by E. Panofsky, *Idea*, Leipzig-Berlin, 1924, p. 115. (Passeri, *Vite de' pittori*, Hess edition, p. 9, does mention the dangers of imitating Michelangelo, but not in connection with the general decline of painting.) The nineteenth century's preoccupation with this has its chief antecedents, on the one hand, in the concern expressed in the sixteenth century about exclusive imitation of one style, especially Michelangelo's, and, on the other, in the view held by some in the sixteenth century that Michelangelo's influence (especially that of his *Last Judgment*) was great but not wholly beneficial, particularly because it led to the widespread use of poses and gestures frequently inappropriate to the subjects painted.

Battisti has recently drawn attention to the rivalry in the sixteenth century between two theories about the way for a writer or painter to form a style: exclusive imitation of one artist and imitation of various good artists. Both had supporters. (See E. Battisti, "Il concetto d'imitazione nel cinquecento da Raffaello a Michelangelo," *Commentari*, VII, 1956, pp. 86 ff.).

Vasari was in favor of forming one's style (one's *maniera* in a sense entirely free of blame) with the help of many models, as Raphael had done (*Le vite de' più eccellenti pittori*, etc., ed. Gaetano Milanesi, Florence, 1875–85, IV, pp. 373 ff.), but he wrote at some length about the danger of imitating one master and of not combining the study of nature with the imitation of style (III, pp. 115–116, discussed below in this footnote). At the same time, he thought exclusive imitation of Michelangelo produced a harsh style full of difficulties, without beauty, without color, and poor in invention. (See Vasari-Milanesi, IV, p. 376. Cf. also Dolce, *Dialogo della pittura*, in Barocchi, *Trattati d'arte*, I, p. 148 and Pietro Aretino in Barocchi, I, p. 438, as well as Antonio Billi, cited by E. Battisti,

"La critica a Michelangelo prima del Vasari," *Rinascimento*, V, 1954, p. 124.) Vasari would not have included among exclusive imitators of Michelangelo either himself or Salviati, whose work he greatly admired and with whom he had systematically studied all the art available in Rome as a young man (Vasari-Milanesi, VII, pp. 13 and 654). Both, however, were painters of the decline in the nineteenth (and seventeenth) century sense. Obviously Vasari did not object to what were, for the nineteenth century, some of the main peculiarities of Cinquecento painting, much less blame them on imitation of Michelangelo.

It is rather the same with Armenini. He gave both theories of imitation. There were two ways of achieving a good *maniera* (in a perfectly laudable sense): one, to draw frequently from the works of good artists; the other, to work only from those of one excellent artist. But he warned that in the second way lay the danger of not being able to imitate one artist fully, of imitating only "one or two parts," not all—with unpleasing, discordant results. In imitating Michelangelo, which was particularly difficult, some, he said, saw the substance and perfection of his art in anatomy and bones, some in muscles, some in poses, some in contours; and in each case they concentrated only on what they considered important. Others thought they could "mix with some parts of [Michelangelo] parts of others" or treat certain elements in a light, pretty way, out of keeping with his style, not realizing "in what respect his manner is difficult and different from all the others." (See Armenini, *De' veri precetti della pittura*, pp. 60, 65 ff.; cf. also Dolce in Barocchi, *op. cit.*, I, pp. 178–179). The notion of uncomprehending imitation is already here. Armenini, unlike Vasari, saw a widespread decline in painting of his time. He complained of confusion and complication in composition and far-fetched eccentric poses (*op. cit.*, pp. 47, 70), but he bemoaned more a general falling off of craft and quality (*ibid.*, pp. 1, 9–18, 130–131). Like Vasari, however, he thoroughly approved of Salviati (*ibid.*, pp. 16–18), who represented decline for the nineteenth (and seventeenth) centuries, and nowhere did he connect the decline that he saw with exclusive imitation of Michelangelo.

For the minority Cinquecento view that Michelangelo "ha data e dà la norma a tutti i pittori che sono ora e che saranno" but that his influence led artists to think only of showing "la forza dell' arte" and to use gestures and strained poses inappropriate to all but fanciful subjects, see Giovanni Andrea Gilio, *Dialogo nel quale si ragiona degli errori e degli abusi de' pittori circa l'istorie*, Camerino, 1564, in Barocchi, *Trattati d'arte*, II, pp. 40, 45–49, 54.

The nineteenth century's association of the exclusive, uncomprehending imitation of previous styles, especially Michelangelo's, with the vice of Mannerism must have developed both from the suggestion of these Cinquecento views (even though the concern about exclusive imitation was not originally expressed apropos of many of the chief peculiarities that the nineteenth century saw in mid-Cinquecento painting) and from the realization at the same time that study and copying of the best works of previous masters was explicitly recommended by Vasari (and Armenini) for gaining *maniera* (even though these writers had used the term in a praiseworthy sense). The association was probably furthered by the criticism that Lomazzo directed, in the later Cinquecento, against painters who, he said, had abandoned their own bent and devoted themselves only to imitating others, working only *per forza d'arte*, so that, having lost their first manner and given themselves to another, they had become worse and worse with time (cited by E. Battisti, "Il concetto d'imitazione nel cinquecento dai veneziani a Caravaggio," *Commentari*, VII, 1956, p. 253).

Recently Battisti has introduced a statement about *maniera* written in the mid-seventeenth century by the sculptor Orfeo Boselli, in which *maniera* is said to be "il modo de l'opperare più ad imitazione di una cosa fatta che di una altra." Boselli adds that the artist can go wrong in doing this, either through his own bad bent, or from imitating bad masters and thereby learning false precepts from the outset, "dalli quali si forma un habito che una volta vestito è difficile a mutarsi." (See E. Battisti, *Rinascimento e barocco*, footnote on pp. 217–218.) Here the Cinquecento idea of forming a good *maniera* with the aid of imitating others has been put into a definition of *maniera* and two dangers pointed out. The word *maniera* thus becomes somewhat stained with the possible ill effects of imitation. And the notion appears that a bad habit can result; but this notion is tied to the imitation of bad masters only.

To my knowledge, there are only two earlier passages in which the word *maniera* is thought to have been used with an unfavorable connotation in connection with the ill effects of imitation: the introduction to Vasari's Life of Mino da Fiesole (Vasari-Milanesi, III, pp. 115–116; cf. the translation by Marco Treves, "*Maniera*, the History of the Word," *op. cit.*, p. 75, and see also S. L. Alpers, "*Ekphrasis* and the Aesthetic Attitudes in Vasari's *Lives*," *Journal of the Warburg and Courtauld Institutes*, XXIII, 1960, p. 214, an article called to my attention by E. H. Gombrich) and a sentence in the life of Giorgione (Vasari-Milanesi, IV, p. 97; cf. Treves, *op. cit.*, p. 76).

As interpreted by Treves and Alpers, the first passage, particularly, would indicate early association of the imitation of others with *maniera* as a vice, and hence support its association in the nineteenth century with Mannerism as a vice.

But is not their interpretation influenced by acquaintance with *maniera's* subsequent connotation as a derogatory term, by the nineteenth century's preoccupation with mannered style as resulting from imitation? Does *maniera* in Vasari's passage really mean anything more than manner in the sense untouched by blame, in the sense more or less of style and good style, usual in Vasari elsewhere (cf. Treves, *op. cit.*, pp. 72–74)? To me, the translation is more likely to be the one given by G. de Vere, *Vasari's Lives of the Painters, Sculptors, and Architects*, London, 1912–1914, III, p. 153. And if instead of translating *maniera* by the word "manner," as De Vere does, we use the word "style," simply in order to eliminate the overtones of "manner" for a modern ear, the meaning De Vere sees in the crucial line becomes still sharper: "For it can be very clearly seen that he seldom passes ahead who always walks behind [cf. Vasari-Milanesi, VII, p. 280]; because the imitation of nature is firm (i.e., firmly fixed) (*è ferma*) in the style of that artist who has turned long practice (*la lunga pratica*) into style (good style)." (Elsewhere Vasari affirms that *maniera*, clearly in a laudable sense, and *giudizio* both develop on the basis of *pratica*: Vasari-Milanesi, VII, p. 427; cf. footnote 38 below.) Vasari goes on: "For imitation [of nature] is a firm art (*una ferma arte*) of doing what you do exactly, according to the most beautiful things of nature, taking her unmixed, without the style of your master or of others, who also reduce the things they take from nature to style ... he who studies closely only styles of artists, and not bodies and natural things, will necessarily render his works less good than nature and than the works of the one from whom he takes his style ... if they [i.e., many artists] had studied both style and natural things *together* [my italics], they would have borne better fruit in their works than they did."

Taken in this same sense, *maniera* in the line on Giorgione is also relieved of stigma. But the way these passages have been read could have helped to cement the eventual association of uncomprehending and mostly exclusive imitation with Mannerism.

27. Ludovico Dolce, *Dialogo della pittura*, in Barocchi, *Trattati d'Arte*, I, p. 196.

28. Vasari-Milanesi, IV, p. 8 and *Le vite del Vasari nell' edizione del 1550*, ed. Corrado Ricci, Milan, n. d., III, p. 4.

29. It seems to me likely that "le cose più belle" means, not simply selections from nature, but also "the choicest ancient and modern works," in view of what Vasari says in Vasari-Milanesi, I, pp. 172–173 and VII, pp. 447–448 (also, for that matter, in III, pp. 115–116, as read in footnote 26) and of what follows in this paper.

30. For the distinction, see Vincenzo Danti, *Il primo libro del trattato delle perfette proporzioni*, Florence, 1567, in Barocchi, *Trattati d'arte*, I, p. 241.

31. For the uses of the term *maniera* with respect to art in the Cinquecento and after, see Panofsky, *Idea*, pp. 114–115; Friedlaender, *Mannerism and Anti-mannerism*, pp. 47 to 48; G. C. Argan, "Maniera e Manierismo," *Enciclopedia italiana*, XXII, 1934, p. 126; A. Blunt, *Artistic Theory in Italy 1450–1600*, Oxford, 1940, pp. 154 ff.; Treves, *op. cit.*, pp. 69 ff. Recent interpretations are given by Luigi Coletti, "Intorno alla storia del concetto di manierismo," *Convivium*, 1948, pp. 801–811; Georg Weise, "*Maniera* und *pellegrino*, zwei Lieblingswörter der italienischen Literatur der Zeit des Manierismus," *Romanistisches Jahrbuch*, III, 1950, pp. 321 ff.; *idem*, "La doppia origine del concetto di manierismo," *Studi vasariani*, Florence, 1952, pp. 181–185; E. Battisti, "Lo spirito del manierismo," *Letteratura*, IV, nos. 21–22, May-August, 1956, pp. 3–10; N. Ivanoff, "Stile e maniera," *Saggi e memorie di storia dell'arte*, Venice, 1957, pp. 109 ff.; and E. Battista, *Rinascimento e barocco*, pp. 219–222. None of these deals with Dolce's use of *maniera* or the part of Vasari's statement given above in italics.

It has been stressed on occasion that for Vasari *maniera* involved idealization: see Argan, *op. cit.*, and also C. L. Ragghianti, "Il valore dell' opera di Giorgio Vasari," *Rendiconti della R. Accademia Nazionale dei Lincei, classe di scienze morali, storiche e filologiche*, series 6, IX, 1933, pp. 780–784.

It is perhaps worth noting that Dvořák, who went farthest in preparing the extreme modern meaning of Mannerism, thought that concern with the meaning of the word *maniera* had been misleading: it applied only to an unimportant aspect of the sixteenth century, but it had been used to evaluate a whole period (cf. *Geschichte der italienischen Kunst*, II, pp. 178, 193).

32. As Mahon has implied that he sees it: cf. *Studies in Seicento Art and Theory*, p. 64.

33. Cf. footnote 6 above.

34. *Ibid.*

35. Even if Vasari's use was new, it had been available since his 1550 edition.

Vasari himself once used *maniera* in connection with repetition in the work of Perugino (Vasari-Milanesi, III, p. 585): "The theory of his art was so reduced to *maniera* ("to style") that he gave all his figures the same look." This usage suggests a point of departure for the development of the derogatory use of *maniera* (vis-à-vis Vasari's *bella maniera*) reported by Dolce.

(Cf. the criticism of Perugino's repetition of figures in Paolo Giovio's *De viris illustribus*, available in Tiraboschi, *Storia della letteratura italiana*, Modena, 1781, IX, p. 262, and Leonardo's insistence on struggling against the habit of repetition in facial types, probably in reaction to the artistic situation of the late Quattrocento, though he considered it a defect natural to any artist, as discussed by E. H. Gombrich, "Leonardo's Grotesque Heads, Prolegomena to their Study," in *Leonardo, saggi e ricerche*, ed. Achille Marazza, Rome, 1954, pp. 209 ff. I am grateful to Professor Gombrich for calling my attention to both of these references.)

36. The opinions of those who have commented on Dolce's use of *maniera* vary as to its implications. Mahon, *Studies in Seicento Art and*

Theory, p. 64, sees a connection with distance from the truth. Mark Roskill, *Dolce's "Aretino" and Venetian Art Theory of the Cinquecento*, unpublished dissertation, Princeton University, 1961, p. 302, says: "The reference seems to be to artists who follow a master by taking over a few of his most prominent figural types and weaving around these an endless series of constructed 'variations'" (i.e., the imitation theory of Mannerism). Luigi Grassi, *Problemi intorno a Michelangelo e il concetto di maniera*, Rome, 1955, p. 9, combines both of these views, interpreting Dolce's *maniera* as "quel 'fare di pratica' che significa allontarsi dalla verità e imitare, invece, la maniera di altri senza spontaneità che era necessaria agli artisti." E. Battisti, "La critica a Michelangelo dopo il Vasari," *Rinascimento*, VII, 1956, p. 151, says that with Dolce *maniera* as *cattiva pratica* is identified with Michelangelo.

Indeed, Michelangelo's later work may not have been exempt from the term in its derogative sense, since Dolce's aside on *maniera* occurs in the discussion of Raphael's variety versus Michelangelo's monotony. Dolce seems to have been thinking chiefly of the *Last Judgment* in the dialogue: see Barocchi, *Trattati d'arte*, I, pp. 188 ff.

37. The contrast between *maniera* and reliance on nature is implied in other Cinquecento uses of the term *maniera*: see Treves, *op. cit.*, pp. 74–76 for this implication in Vasari and Vasari-Milanesi, III, pp. 115–116, discussed in footnote 26 above. Armenini's use of *maniera* is likely to carry approximately the same meaning as Vasari's, it seems to me, and it, too, implies the same contrast: see his criticism of those who paint nudes "tuttavia di pura maniera" —meaning evidently "on the basis always of *maniera* (of style) alone without reference again to the living model" —and his warning elsewhere that "con la sola maniera non si può supplire al tutto"; Armenini. *De' veri precetti*, pp. 131 and 223–224. (For important instances of Armenini's use of *maniera*, see also pp. 59, 60–61, and 88–89.)

38. *Pratica* implies routine in, for example, Vasari-Milanesi, VI, pp. 382, 397, and 588; it implies the practised hand in I, pp. 169, 171, IV, p. 113, and VII, pp. 427 and 431 as well as in passages cited below in footnote 170. In Dolce's passage the meaning of *pratica* seems to be procedure, with an overtone of routine procedure. Elsewhere Dolce used *pratica* in the sense of reliance on routine pro-

cedure without reference to the best in nature: see Barocchi, *Trattati d'arte*, I, p. 172.

Vasari suggests that both *maniera* (in the praiseworthy sense) and *giudizio* develop with *pratica:* see Vasari-Milanesi, VII, p. 427. (Cf. also III, p. 115, as translated in footnote 26 above.) Armenini gives the impression that he thought exclusive reliance on *maniera* involved reliance on *pratica* and also on *idea* (see footnote 42 below). Bellori was to say that *maniera* was based on *pratica* (see footnote 6). See also Giustiniani in footnote 16. For the association of *maniera* and *pratica*, see Treves, *op. cit.*, p. 76.

39. See the two articles cited in footnote 31. But as in the translation of *maniera* in reference to painting (see below, footnote 40), so in its translation in reference to deportment, "style" may be a more salutary word to use than "artificiality."

40. Treves, *op. cit.*, p. 75, considers *maniera* came to mean stylization on occasion in Vasari. The passages he cites as examples are Vasari-Milanesi, III, pp. 115 and 585 and IV, p. 97, in all of which, as I have suggested, the word "style" seems the more just translation: see footnotes 26 and 35 above.

Indeed, "style" seems to me always the preferable translation for *maniera* in Vasari, especially in order to avoid letting later implications of the word "manner" prejudice his meaning for us.

Similarly in the case of Dolce's derogatory *maniera*, I think we get its flavor if we try to imagine the word "style" used deprecatingly or scornfully.

It will help in the discussion that follows to remind ourselves continually that *maniera* can be translated as "style," whether we want its affirmative or derogatory meaning.

If we translate Vasari's and Dolce's *maniera* simply as "style" and Bellori's as "the style," I believe we make a helpful and justifiable distinction, however slight, between Vasari's and Dolce's uses of the word for what they saw in painting of their own moment (each from his own point of view) and Bellori's retrospective use of it for a phenomenon in painting of the previous century.

41. There is no suggestion of this in Dolce's words on *maniera* or elsewhere in the dialogue. He directed much criticism against tend-

encies that were most in evidence in *maniera* as described in this paper: over-stressed, far-fetched movement, as he thought, too much foreshortening, cursory contours, reliance on routine procedure, lack of variety, too much finish and embellishment of figures. He considered these wearisome and bad. But he did not lay them to the capricious imagination of artists. (See Dolce in Barocchi, *Trattati d'arte*, I, pp. 176–185.)

42. *Idea* is considered to have in Vasari almost the meaning of imagination (cf. Panofsky, *Idea*, p. 34). The notion of a relation between *maniera* and *idea* is an old one. Armenini gives the impression that he believed exclusive reliance on *maniera* involved reliance, not only on *pratica*, but on *idea* (*De' veri precetti*, pp. 223–224). Bellori seems to equate *maniera* and *fantastica idea*. And only recently *maniera* and *idea* have been considered almost identical (Battisti, *Lo spirito del manierismo*, p. 5 and *idem*, *Rinascimento e barocco*, p. 220). It is worth asking, then, what Vasari's view may have been of the relation of *maniera*, and *bella maniera*, to *idea* and what his conception of *idea* tells about *maniera* and imagination.

Vasari indicates that *idea* imagines inventions (Vasari-Milanesi, VII, p. 427). At the same time, as I tend to interpret his difficult introductory passage (*idem*, I, pp. 168–169), *idea* seems to serve as an ideal standard of judgment in the artist's mind with respect to all things in nature and art, especially as to relationships of proportion. (As I am inclined to read him in these passages, it is distinct from the artistic conception of the specific work of art.) And according to Panofsky (*Idea*, p. 33), Vasari's *idea* derives from the artist's experience of reality.

Hence, while Vasari would doubtless agree that the relation of *maniera*, and *bella maniera*, to *idea* was one of dependence, his *idea* does not appear to be capricious imagination in disregard of truth to nature. (For the problem of Vasari's concept both of *idea* and of its origin in the artist's mind, see Panofsky, *Idea*, pp. 33 ff.; the proposal in Walter Friedlaender's review of Panofsky's book, *Jahrbuch für Kunstwissenschaft*, 1928, pp. 56–64; R. W. Lee, "*Ut pictura poesis:* the Humanistic theory of Painting," *Art Bulletin*, XXII, 1940, p. 207; E. Battisti, "Il concetto d'imitazione nel cinquecento da Raffaello a Michelangelo," *Commentari*, VII, 1956, p. 92, where Pico's Idea of eloquence is defined as an almost instinctive criterion of choice—

somewhat comparable, I should think, to Vasari's in painting, but more inspired; and *ibid.*, pp. 100 ff.)

43. While it became one of the main grounds for criticizing *maniera* (see footnote 6), the view that painting *di maniera* depends primarily on the artist's fancy appears first, so far as I know, in Giustiniani's letter (see footnote 16) without an expression of disapproval. Doubtless it was encouraged by preoccupation with the subjective aspect of the creative process in the second half of the Cinquecento and early Seicento (described by Panofsky, *Idea*, pp. 44–56; cf. also Gerald Ackermann, "Gian Battista Marino's Contribution to Seicento Theory," *Art Bulletin*, XLIII, 1961, pp. 332–333. I am grateful to the author for letting me read his article in advance of publication). But its retention as part of the indictment of *maniera* must have been favored by the Seicento's lack of understanding of *maniera's* basis as sketched below in this paper.

44. See footnote 6 above. Obviously, however, opinion against aspects of mid-Cinquecento painting other than monotonous uniformity had begun to appear in the sixteenth century itself: witness Dolce (footnote 41 above) and Gilio, *Dialogo... degli errori e degli abusi de' pittori circa l'istorie*, in Barocchi, *Trattati d'arte*, II, pp. 3–4.

The monotonous aspect of *maniera* comes to the fore again in later criticism. Cf. de Piles' remark on line 233 of the Latin text of Du Fresnoy on the art of painting, as given in *The Art of Painting by C. A. Du Fresnoy with Remarks: translated into English... by Mr. Dryden*, London, 1716, p. 157: "And it is that Diversity of Species which distinguishes these Painters who are able artists, from those whom we may call Mannerists, and who repeat five or six times over in the same picture the same airs of the head." Part of Milizia's definition also stays close to Dolce. First he says: "One calls the affected *ammanierato*. Affectation is a very bad imitation of simplicity, naturalness, nobility, graces. One is *ammanierato* by excess, if one exaggerates and enlarges, or by lack, if one makes small, or by impropriety of forms, dispositions, expression, colors, etc." But then he adds: "One is also *ammanierato* through frequent repetition of the same things. Nature is infinite in its modifications." (F. Milizia, *Dizionario delle belle arti del disegno*, Bologna, 1827 [originally published 1787] II, p. 197.)

45. Vasari-Milanesi, IV, pp. 8–15.

46. For a recent interpretation of Vasari's introduction somewhat different from the one here, cf. Lionello Venturi, "La critica di Giorgio Vasari," *Studi vasariani*, Florence, 1952, pp. 29 ff. M. Rosci, "Manierismo e accademismo nel pensiero critico del cinquecento," *Acme*, IX, no. 1, 1956, p. 66, sees this introduction as an unequaled contemporary source concerning the style of Mannerism, but he seems to be thinking of early Mannerism and considers that Vasari's analysis reduces it academically to formal schemes (rather as painters like Vasari are thought to have reduced early Mannerism in imitating it).

For the aims and methods of *maniera* painting, Armenini is also invaluable, even though he had begun to see faults connected with it (cf. footnote 26 above). Lomazzo painted in the *maniera* vein, but as a writer he seems a less reliable witness for *maniera*. It is as if, when he wrote, he had been touched with the spirit of reform, even in his discussions of movement. But see J. Schlosser, *La letteratura artistica*, Florence, 1935, pp. 344–345 for another view.

To supplement Vasari's statement, one should remember that he ranked Salviati especially high among painters.

47. For Vasari's concept of grace as an indefinable quality dependent on judgment, see A. Blunt, *Artistic Theory in Italy*, pp. 93–98. Cf. Varchi in Barocchi, *Trattati d'arte*, I, pp. 85–91; also Vincenzo Danti, *ibid.*, pp. 228–230, where grace is connected especially with attitudes and movements; and K. Birch-Hirschfeld, *Die Lehre von der Malerei. Ein Beitrag zur Geschichte der Malerei des Cinquecento*, Leipzig, 1912, p. 40.

48. See also Vasari-Milanesi, IV, pp. 373–377.

49. See also *ibid.*, p. 375.

50. The passage on speed was one of the few additions to the introduction in the edition of 1568. Cf. also Vasari, I, p. 173. For the background of this ideal, see Robert J. Clements, "Michelangelo on Effort and Rapidity in Art," *Journal of the Warburg and Courtauld Institutes*, XVII, 1954, pp. 301–310; Blunt, *op. cit.*, pp. 95–98;

Rosci, *Manierismo e accademismo nel pensiero critico del cinquecento*, pp. 62–64; also Barocchi, *Trattati d'arte*, I, pp. 472–473.

51. Vasari-Milanesi, VII, p. 210. Vasari makes clear in the rest of this passage on the *Last Judgment*, from which the quotation comes, that Michelangelo chose to omit from his painting elements that Vasari himself approved. These coincide with those he has given in the introduction to Part III. See also Vasari-Milanesi, I, pp. 177–178.

52. See also L. Venturi, *La critica di Giorgio Vasari*, p. 42; R. Scrivano, *Il manierismo nella letteratura del cinquecento*, Padua, 1959, pp. 40 ff. (he sees Vasari as optimistic about the future); and S. L. Alpers, "*Ekphrasis* and Aesthetic Attitudes in Vasari's *Lives*," *Journal of the Warburg and Courtauld Institutes*, XIII, 1960, pp. 204–209 (called to my attention by E. H. Gombrich), where it is argued that Vasari's concept of perfection refers to the perfection of representational means and that he did not expect a necessary decline "nor some kind of lesser, more widespread perfection" in the future. See also Gombrich's view that Vasari saw tasks for painting that would save it from decline: E. H. Gombrich, "Recent Concepts of Mannerism, the Historiographic Background," *op. cit.* But see, too, J. Schlosser, *La letteratura artistica*, p. 273, for the contrary opinion.

It is worth stressing that Vasari was highly praised in his own time: E. Steinmann, "Freskenzyklen der Spätrenaissance in Rom," *Monatshefte für Kunstwissenschaft*, 1906, pp. 45 ff. An indication of what contemporaries valued in Vasari's kind of painting is given by the letter of Doni to Lelio Torelli describing Vasari's frescoes in the Cancellaria, in which some qualities are lauded that Vasari stressed in the introduction to Part III in the *Lives:* see Bottari and Ticozzi, *Raccolta di lettere*, V, pp. 149–162, especially p. 161.

53. Weisbach, *Der Manierismus*, especially pp. 164–166, 170–171; H. Voss, *Die Malerei der Spätrenaissance*, Berlin, 1920, I, pp. 5, 147–148, 209 ff., 278–280 and II, pp. 302, 342, and 436 for example; W. Pinder, *Die deutsche Plastik vom ausgehenden Mittelalter bis zum Ende der Renaissance*, Berlin, 1914–1929, pp. 252 ff.; Pevsner and Grautoff, *Die Barockmalerei in den romanischen Ländern*, pp. 5 ff., 44; F. Antal, "Zum Problem des niederländischen Manierismus,"

Kritische Berichte, III/IV, 1928/1929, pp. 213 ff. Except for Voss, who confined the term Mannerism to painting from Vasari and Salviati on, it can be said of all these that they tended to characterize both early Mannerism and mature Mannerism more in terms of painting after 1530 than before, in contrast to Friedlaender, for instance: hence their observations on the conventions, and hence also Antal's tendency, for example, to select for comment from the 'twenties the works that most anticipate later ones.

See also Dvořák, *Geschichte der italienischen Kunst*, II, pp. 119, 128, 131, 140–143, where there is a considerable distinction between earlier and later phases; Hoffmann, *Hochrenaissance, Manierismus, Frühbarock, passim*, where there is an awareness of most of the conventions, though the emphasis is on other matters, especially space; E. K. Waterhouse, *Baroque Painting in Rome*, London, 1937; and E. Panofsky, *What is Baroque?* mimeographed summary of a lecture of the middle 1930's, available at the Institute of Fine Arts, New York University, with acute observations, to which I am indebted.

54. And obviously it was countered in some degree by the differentiation required by *decorum*.

55. See Armenini, *De' veri precetti*, pp. 81 ff. The principle of *maniera* light has not been remarked upon, to my knowledge. In a lecture in 1943 Millard Meiss characterized the light in "Neo-Gothic" painting of the fifteenth century as the property of planes that parallel the picture plane. I have no doubt that this observation helped prepare me to see the rather comparable phenomenon in *maniera*. Below I suggest that the two phenomena are related as to origin: see footnote 191.

56. In *maniera* is the climax of the Central Italian stress on the action, extension, and disposition of the body's members, which has deep roots in theory (cf. Leon Battista Alberti, *Della pittura*, ed. Luigi Mallé, Florence, Sansoni, 1950, pp. 89–90) and in later fifteenth century painting. But it is worth noting that *maniera's* accentuation of limbs is one of its differences from what we are apt to consider some of the purest High Renaissance painting—Raphael's *Disputà*, for example, or Ridolfo Ghirlandaio's *Translation of the Body of Saint*

53

Zenobius. Accented limbs were not part of the High Renaissance classic ideal in its most natural vein.

57. The Cinquecento's terms *sforzi* and *sforzati* for difficult figures reflect the desirability of strain, relating chiefly to the twists of the body and its members. Cf. Pino in Barocchi, *Trattati d'arte*, I, p. 115, where "sforziata" is linked with the words "misteriosa" and "difficile" to describe a praiseworthy figure that proves an artist "valente," or Dolce in Barocchi, I, p. 180; cf. also, however, Gilio's disapproval of *sforzi* when used inappropriately: *Degli errori de' pittori* in Barocchi, II, pp. 4, 33, 46, etc.

58. My awareness of the importance of this spotting I owe to comments by Leo Steinberg in a seminar.

59. See Voss, *Die Malerei der Spätrenaissance*, I, p. 191, fig. 59 for another example.

60. As I discovered simply in keeping track of poses. Cf. the diagrammatic devices for showing the body in various positions found in drawing books, which began to appear exactly in the period of *maniera* for the purpose of teaching the vocabulary of painting and to which attention has recently been drawn by E. H. Gombrich, *Art and Illusion*, New York, 1959, pp. 157–168 and figs. 118 and 129.

61. Cf. the criticisms of Dolce in Barocchi, *Trattati d'arte*, I, p. 171; Gilio in Barocchi, II, pp. 46–48; or Armenini, *De' veri precetti*, p. 70.

62. See the passage quoted by Ivanoff, *Stile e maniera*, p. 122.

63. Carel van Mander, *Het Leven der Doorluchtighe Nederlandtsche en Hooghduytsche Schilders*, ed. Hanns Floerke, Munich and Leipzig, 1906, I, pp. 294–297. He was critical of the Italians for this, especially the mediocre ones. They did not go into details or bother their heads with the study of muscles, sinews, and blood vessels; and the result was dry.

64. But this lent itself to the calligraphy important in *maniera*.
Baldinucci's criticism (*Notizie de' professori*, XXI, pp. 120–122, from a lecture delivered in 1691) was directed precisely against lack

of truth to the complexity and variety of the body's formation. He affirmed that the members and muscles were diverse among themselves and made possible an infinite variety of motions and actions. In their many movements the muscles—and the passage from one muscle to another—took an infinite variety of shapes. The artist's hand should be so obedient that it could carry the stylus through the continually varied, difficult paths necessary to represent this complexity and variety. Defect in this regard was due to "weakness of intelligence and, even more, of the hand in obeying the truth," and the defect was called *maniera* or *ammanierato*. Nearly every painter showed something of it; Baldinucci could cite only Michelangelo, Raphael, and Andrea del Sarto as examples for draftsmen to follow.

Baldinucci was concerned here with an aspect of *maniera's* disregard of nature that is not brought out in most other Seicento sources or elsewhere by Baldinucci himself. It continues, in a sense, the Cinquecento association of *maniera* with lack of variety in the human figure as reported by Dolce.

65. In drawings, the conventions of contour and modeling or simply contour can sometimes be enough to make one want to classify a work as belonging to *maniera*, even when other conventions are little in evidence.

66. Vasari-Milanesi, I, pp. 173, 179–181 and Armenini, *De' veri precetti*, pp. 106–107. Vasari indicated that lively colors were undesirable also because they interfered with *disegno* and relief.

67. Cf. also Armenini, *De' veri precetti*, pp. 127–128, 130, 132.

68. Generally involving *morbidezza*, mentioned often as desirable (cf. Rouchette, *La renaissance que nous a léguée Vasari*, p. 388 and Blunt, *Artistic Theory in Italy*, p. 94). To judge by Baldinucci, it must have meant delicate fleshiness, even though in sculpturesque terms, and the opposite of the coarse and rough (cf. F. Baldinucci, *Vocabulario toscana dell' arte del disegno*, Florence, 1681, p. 100).

69. Cf. footnote 168 below.
Besides the quick sketch (see Armenini, *op. cit.*, pp. 55, 72–75, 138) there was, of course, the finished drawing, where the finishing of contours was especially important (*ibid.*, pp. 53–54, 77, 138).

70. Cf. Lee, *op. cit.*, pp. 217 ff.

71. Among which one can perhaps put the ambiguity originating in the contradiction between the convention of flatness and the inordinate Cinquecento interest in foreshortening (particularly as a demonstration of the painter's ability, whereas once *scorti* had been attractive more especially for their help in giving depth).

72. Vasari's words on Iacone's efforts to vary poses are illuminating: see Vasari-Milanesi, VI, p. 450.

73. For observations on the continual use of antique subjects as a basis for formal problems but the decline of deep interest in them, see Fritz Saxl, *Antike Götter in der Spätrenaissance*, Studien der Bibliothek Warburg, VIII, Leipzig and Berlin, 1927, pp. 25–26, 30.

74. For an earlier formulation of the relationship of *maniera* to Roman relief stated here, see C. H. Smyth, *Bronzino Studies*, dissertation, Princeton University, 1955, pp. 252 ff.

75. A. Riegl, *Spätrömische Kunstindustrie*, Vienna, 1927, pp. 127 ff., 139 ff., and 144 ff.
    In my Figures 14 and 15 it will be seen that the former represents the more *maniera*-like tendencies in pose and in that combination of flatness with turning and movement in depth that suggests the need of freedom, while the latter represents a more straight-forward flatness.

76. In this connection, we may also note characteristic movements of the limbs that *maniera* shares with many Roman reliefs, such as the arm crossing the chest (cf. Fig. 17) or raised in the air (cf. Fig. 14). Vasari must, I think, have had this sort of movement of limbs in mind when he characterized the movement in antique figures that influenced Cinquecento painters, to judge from his own painting and his wording of the passage in question (Vasari-Milanesi, IV, p. 10, quoted earlier in the present essay on page 8).

77. Cf. K. Lehmann-Hartleben and Erling C. Olsen, *Dionysiac Sarcophagi in Baltimore*, 1942, p. 60; also pp. 77–78, 81, and illustrations.

78. Cf. footnote 82 below.

79. See footnote 6.

80. See Armenini, *De' veri precetti*, pp. 49–50, 57, 58, 61 (and the partial translations of two of these passages in R. Goldwater and M. Treves, *Artists on Art*, New York, 1945, pp. 108–109).

81. Armenini, *op. cit.*, p. 58.

82. *Ibid.*, p. 88.

83. *Ibid.*, pp. 57–58.

84. Vasari-Milanesi, I, p. 172. See, in addition, *ibid.*, pp. 170 and 241–242 for Vasari's opinion that the Renaissance in art came from imitating antique sculpture, of which he names especially reliefs. Cf. also Paola Barocchi, "Il valore dell' antico nella storiografia vasariana," *Convegno internazionale sul rinascimento*, V, Florence, 1956, pp. 217–236.

Dolce would not have disputed the importance of antique models, but, as he evidently saw it, the variety he valued in Raphael and wanted to see in others came from combining study from life with "imitation of the *bella maniera* of antique statues" . . . "in modo che, veggendo le cose dal vivo, dava loro più bella forma, ricercando nelle sue opere una perfezione intera che non si trova nel vivo . . ." And he warned specifically that judgment was needed to imitate in the antique the good parts and not the bad. See the letter of Ludovico Dolce to Gaspero Ballini in Bottari and Ticozzi, *Raccolta di lettere*, V, p. 171; Barocchi, *Trattati d'arte*, I, p. 176; and Lee, *op. cit.*, p. 205.

85. See Vasari's praise of the *maniera* of Giulio Romano as "sempre anticamente moderna, et modernamente antica" (Vasari-Ricci, IV, p. 327), coinciding with Aretino's words in a letter to Giulio of 1542 (cf. F. Pertile and E. Camesasca, *Lettere sull' arte di Pietro Aretino*, Milan, 1957–1960, I, p. 215, III, part 2, p. 512 and E. H. Gombrich, "Zum Werke Giulio Romanos," *Jahrbuch der kunsthistorischen Sammlungen in Wien*, N. F., IX, 1935, p. 125).

Vasari himself received this very praise for the garments in his most characteristically *maniera* work, the frescoes of the Cancelleria: "...abiti modernamente antichi, ed anticamente moderni, che dimostrano il grande ingegno del pittore," in the letter of Doni to Lelio Torelli (Bottari and Ticozzi, *Raccolta di lettere*, V, p. 161). Cf. also Vasari-Milanesi, VI, p. 298 and Rouchette, *La renaissance que nous a léguée Vasari*, pp. 98–100.

86. Cf. in this connection the parallel, brought out by Battisti, between Bembo's ideal of imitation in writing as the reproduction of the totality of the style of one's model and Bembo's description of the way Cinquecento artists study and imitate antiquities in their own work (Battisti, *Il concetto d'imitazione nel cinquecento da Raffaello a Michelangelo*, pp. 96–97).

87. David R. Coffin, *The Villa d'Este at Tivoli*, Princeton, 1960, pp. 76–77. Ligorio's similarity to Vasari as a *maniera* artist is close (though Coffin believes he has nothing to do with the Florentine School).

For the suggestion that spatial abstraction in Roman relief reinforced similar tendencies in Cinquecento painting, see P. Bober as cited in footnote 107 below. For a specific instance of probable influence, see footnote 209 below.

88. This will form part of Mrs. Grippi's dissertation on the development of *maniera* poses, now in preparation for New York University. She is publishing shortly an article on the use of specific antique poses and gestures in *maniera*. Her conclusions have added to my understanding of the antique-*maniera* relationship, and I am grateful to her for the examples included in this paper. The photographic illustrations of them, which I showed when the present essay was given as a paper at the XXth Congress, will be reproduced in her article.

For developments leading to the characteristic *maniera* use of antique poses, see the paper delivered at this Congress by E. H. Gombrich, "The Style *all' 'antica:* Imitation and Assimilation," *Acts of the XXth International Congress of the History of Art, Studies of Western Art*, Princeton University Press, forthcoming, volume III. As he says, there is no overlap between the results there and here, but a pleasant accord.

89. See S. Reinach, *Répertoire de reliefs grecs et romains*, III, Paris, 1912, p. 67 (1); Alinari photo P. I. N. 11181. In the sixteenth century it was at the Villa Madama: see C. Hülsen and H. Egger, *Die römischen Skizzenbücher von Martin von Heemskerck im königlichen Kupferstichkabinett zu Berlin*, Berlin, 1913, p. 22 and pl. 41.

90. See Georg Lippold, *Die Skulpturen des vaticanischen Museums*, III, 2, Berlin, 1956, pl. 149, no. 85. Anderson photo 1445.

91. See Andrea Emiliani, *Il Bronzino*, Busto Arsizio, 1960, p. 81 or L. Becherucci, *Bronzino*, Milan-Florence, 1952, pls. 60–61.

92. Part of the decoration in the Palazzo Ricci-Sacchetti, Rome; see P. Bucarelli, "Tesori d'arte nei palazzi romani, gli affreschi di Francesco Salviati nel Palazzo Sacchetti," *Capitolium*, IX, 1933, illustration on p. 249. (I owe the proper identification of the scene to Althea Bradbury, *The System of Mural Decoration of Salviati and his Contemporaries*, unpublished thesis, New York University, 1958, pp. 136–137 and Iris H. Cheney, *Francesco Salviati (1510–1563)*, unpublished dissertation, New York University, 1962.)

93. Florence, Palazzo Vecchio, Salone del Dugento; Alinari photo 46442.

94. See G. S. Adelmann and G. Weise, *Das Fortleben gotischer Ausdrucks- und Bewegungsmotive in der Kunst des Manierismus*, Tübingen, 1954, p. 25, figs. 120–125.

95. See Lehmann-Hartleben and Olsen, *Dionysiac Sarcophagi in Baltimore*, fig. 2, the third figure from the right. Mrs. Grippi points to the antique as ultimately the common source for both the Late Gothic and *maniera* examples.

96. For the Naples sarcophagus, see Phyllis Bober, *Drawings after the Antique by Amico Aspertini, Sketchbooks in the British Museum*, London, 1957, fig. 13, the dancing figure just to the right of the center group. There are two Raimondi prints: A. Bartsch, *Le peintre graveur*, Leipzig, 1867, XIV, pp. 201–202, nos. 248, 249, and a copy by Enea Vico in reverse, Bartsch, XV, p. 298, no. 33. The

sarcophagus was in Rome in the Cinquecento; see P. Bober, *op. cit.*, p. 51.

97. See E. H. Gombrich, "Apollonio di Giovanni, a Florentine Workshop Seen through the Eyes of a Humanist Poet," *Journal of the Warburg and Courtauld Institutes*, XVIII, 1955, pp. 23–24 and L. D. Ettlinger, "Pollaiuolo's Tomb of Pope Sixtus IV," *ibid.*, XVI, 1953, p. 250.

As for the open quotation of figures, it was not new, nor was it confined to those from the antique. Middeldorf has pointed out that the practice of obvious classical citation has a history going back into the fifteenth century: see U. Middeldorf, "Su alcuni bronzetti all' antica del quattrocento," *Il mondo antico nel rinascimento, Atti del V. Convegno internazionale di studi sul rinascimento* (Florence, 1956), Florence, 1958, p. 168. See also P. Bober, *op. cit.*, pp. 21 and 25 and R. Krautheimer with T. Krautheimer-Hess, *Lorenzo Ghiberti*, Princeton, 1956, pp. 277 ff., concerning such quotations at the outset of the fifteenth century. For an outstanding example, in the earlier Cinquecento, of quotation from modern works, see Bacchiacca and the essay by Howard S. Merritt, "Francesco Ubertini called il Bacchiacca, 1494–1557," in *Bacchiacca and his Friends*, an Exhibition Presented by the Baltimore Museum of Art, Jan. 10 to Feb. 19, 1961, *News Quarterly*, Baltimore Museum of Art, XXIV, No. 2, 1961, pp. 19–34. An instance of mid-Cinquecento interest in quotation from earlier masters of the century has been stressed by Webster Smith, *A Study of the Book of Hours for Cardinal Alessandro Farnese in the Pierpont Morgan Library*, unpublished thesis, New York University, 1955, dealing with Clovio's illustrations. Cf. also Briganti, *Il manierismo e Pellegrino Tibaldi*, p. 30.

Whether a source was modern or ancient, quotation must have been engaged in at least partly to satisfy a sophisticated interest in recognizing the origin of a pose and seeing a new inventive use (cf. Smith, *op. cit.*, pp. 74–75).

98. See Michelangelo's letter to Benedetto Varchi in Barocchi, *Trattati d'arte*, I, p. 82 (cf. also F. A. Doni, *Disegno*, Venice, 1549, p. 40).

99. See Barocchi, I, p. 63 (cf. also p. 61).

100. Cf. the similar view of painting versus sculpture in the *Imagines* of Philostratus at the opening of Book I, called to my attention by E. H. Gombrich, who says that L. D. Ettlinger once pointed out to him convincingly that this is the source for the *paragone* altogether. See *Philostratus Imagines, Callistratus Descriptions*, tr. Arthur Fairbanks, London and New York, Loeb Classical Library, 1931, pp. 2–5. (Cf. also Alpers, *"Ekphrasis" and Aesthetic Attitudes in Vasari's "Lives"*, p. 198.)

101. Cf. the inescapable descriptive element in Roman state relief beginning with the second century A.D., of which the Column of Trajan was the first great example. (I am indebted to Karl Lehmann's remarks on the history of Roman relief in lectures on Roman sculpture at New York University in 1952, which I attended because of my interest in the antique-*maniera* connections I suggest.)

There is an indication in the *Lives* that Vasari considered abundance of garments and bizarre fancies had their relation to antiquity: see Vasari-Milanesi, III, p. 461.

For another view on the reasons behind the great interest in detail in *maniera* painting, see Coffin, *Villa d'Este*, p. 77.

102. See footnote 8 above.

Cf. also Milanesi's mention (Vasari-Milanesi, VII, p. 724) of the "servile imitazione degli antichi marmi, nei quali, più che nella natura, credevano, a quella età, fosse il solo tipo imitabile della bellezza."

103. Dvořák, *Geschichte der italienischen Kunst*, II, pp. 123 ff., saw the Raphael School as seeking refuge in the antique, as more archaelogically truthful, and as inspired by it to small poetic narrative and ideal landscape with staffage. On the other hand, it is his view that in the *Last Judgment* the antique is vanquished as a source of inspiration; *ibid.*, p. 127 (but cf. *ibid.*, p. 134). See also pp. 198–199.

104. F. Antal, "Observations on Girolamo da Carpi," *Art Bulletin*, XXX, 1948, p. 98.

105. Werner Weisbach, *Zum Problem des Manierismus*, p. 17, with a reference to Dolce's similar observation (cf. Barocchi, *Trattati d'arte*,

I, p. 176). Weisbach saw the sympathy of Mannerism for the antique, though not the relation to the antique of the main *maniera* conventions of the figure.

106. Adolf Goldschmidt, "Lambert Lombard," *Jahrbuch der preussischen Kunstsammlungen*, XL, 1919, pp. 206 ff.

Cf. also the brief, relevant observation that the "dogmatically antiquarian character" of Bertoldo's battle relief "gives all too clear an indication of the fate that was to overtake Italian art when the antique manner had been correctly understood" in K. Clark, *The Nude, A Study in Ideal Form*, New York, 1956, pp. 202–203.

107. P. Bober, *Drawings after the Antique by Amico Aspertini*, pp. 24–26, especially her concluding observations on p. 26 that "from the study of its [i.e., Roman relief's] spatial abstractions and spiritual agitation comes further reinforcement of contemporary tendencies." See also p. 27 for her excellent description, giving substance to Antal's remark, of the way in which Roman relief style of the late second and early third centuries "embodies some of the conflicting tendencies that appear in Mannerism of the sixteenth century." (She also sees, however, "revived medievalism" in Mannerism, in connection apparently with a characteristic work of *maniera*, Bronzino's *Descent into Limbo*; see p. 25).

Aspertini is Mrs. Bober's one specific example, although she does not classify him as a genuine Mannerist. His study of Antonine and Late Antonine relief did not, in her view, condition the "so-called Mannerism" of his paintings, but reinforced his inherent, capricious disposition and his Quattrocento tendencies, heightening "characteristics present in his work from the outset" into "fortuitously 'Mannerist' features" (pp. 26 ff., especially pp. 27 and 38). Cf. footnote 118 below.

108. While Vasari's contour and modeling coincided with *maniera* ideals from early on (see the *Deposition* of 1532 in V. Baldini, "La *Deposizione* di Giorgio Vasari per il Cardinale Ippolito dei Medici," *Rivista d'arte*, XXVII, 1951–1952, figure on p. 196), *maniera* conventions of posing the figure first begin to make a definite appearance, among his surviving works, in the *Deposition* of 1537 at Arezzo. (For the date, the influence of Rosso's *Transfiguration* on the most pro-

nounced pose, and an illustration, see Bernice F. Davidson, "Vasari's *Deposition* at Arezzo," *Art Bulletin*, XXXVI, 1954, pp. 228–231). The following year, pale *maniera* color first appears in the *Assumption* at Montesansovino, which Vasari thought he had painted "con alquanto migliore maniera" as the result of a spring visit in Rome devoted to study (Vasari-Milanesi, VII, pp. 662–663 and VIII, p. 272), but there are only slight concessions to *maniera* conventions of pose. (Contracted for in December, 1537; see A. Del Vita, *Il libro delle ricordanze di Giorgio Vasari*, Arezzo, 1938, p. 29, where the date "1538" is an error. Photographs made for me of pictures by Vasari at Montesansovino, Arezzo, and Camaldoli should be available through the Gabinetto fotografico, Soprintendenza alle Gallerie, Florence.) Otherwise, there is little or nothing of out-and-out *maniera* in his work of the 'thirties, whether in the conservative *Sacra Conversazione* for San Rocco in Arezzo, now in the museum (ordered and the first sketch made in 1535 but evidently not executed until 1537; see *Ricordanze*, pp. 24, 28 and Vasari-Milanesi, VII, pp. 659 to 660), the *Madonna with Saints John and Jerome* at Camaldoli of 1537 (*Ricordanze*, p. 28, Vasari-Milanesi, VII, p. 661), the dated nocturnal *Nativity* at Camaldoli from the latter part of 1538 (*Ricordanze*, p. 30, Vasari-Milanesi, VII, p. 663), or the two surviving pictures of 1539–1540 for San Michele in Bosco at Bologna: the *Christ in the House of Mary and Martha* at San Michele and the *Supper of Saint Gregory* in the Pinacoteca, Bologna (*Ricordanze*, pp. 31–32, Vasari-Milanesi, VII, pp. 664 ff.). (*Abraham Receiving the Angels*, from San Michele and formerly in the Brera, was destroyed in the war, and no photograph, it seems, was ever made of it.)

For Vasari's paintings in the 'thirties, see also Paola Barocchi, "Il Vasari pittore," *Rinascimento*, VII, 1956, pp. 187 ff.

109. The Camaldoli *Deposition* was commissioned in June, 1539 and sketched then, but not executed until the summer of 1540 (*Ricordanze*, p. 33). The *Immaculate Conception* for SS. Apostoli was done between October, 1540 and September, 1541 (*ibid.*, p. 34).

110. Voss, *Die Malerei der Spätrenaissance*, I, fig. 40. Similarly, Salviati in the same year; see Michael Hirst, "Francesco Salviati's *Visitation*," *Burlington Magazine*, CIII, 1961, pp. 236 ff., for the sources of this important picture from the early phase of the new

development. (In addition to the influences he enumerates and to that of the antique, to be discussed by Mrs. Grippi, I wonder whether, in this picture, Salviati had Flemish tapestries in mind — thanks possibly to acquaintance with Heemskerck or Coxie in Rome.)

111. Voss, *Die Malerei der Spätrenaissance*, I, p. 210, saw the early 1530's as a turning point in style, and Pevsner considered mature Mannerism began then: see Pevsner and Grautoff, *Barockmalerei in den romanischen Ländern*, p. 40.

112. See below, p. 22.

113. For this new date, see Andrea Emiliani, *Il Bronzino*, the notes opposite pls. 34 and 35.

114. Cf. Domenico Veneziano's *Stigmatization of St. Francis* in Washington and Benedetto da Maiano's *Stigmatization* on the pulpit in Santa Croce.

115. The same difference in treatment is found in the preparatory drawing in Frankfurt: between the fluid, illusionistic *Stigmatization*, in which luminary and atmospheric relations are surprisingly brought out and the contours are limber and sensitive to the natural form, and the *Saint Michael*, where the very different, less differentiating contours accentuate the contrast of the two compartments. (Poorly illustrated in Franzsepp Würtenberger, "Die manieristische Deckenmalerei in Mittelitalien," *Römisches Jahrbuch für Kunstgeschichte*, IV, 1940, p. 75.)

116. For some in Central Italy, see F. Zeri, *Pittura e controriforma, l'arte senza tempo di Scipione da Gaeta*, Turin, 1957, especially pp. 45 ff.

117. Varying not only from artist to artist, but sometimes from work to work as in Bronzino's case above. For another example of the latter, see the comparison between Jacopino del Conte's relatively free drawing for the *Deposition* in San Giovanni Decollato and the painting itself as noted by E. Panofsky, "Ein Bildentwurf des Jacopino del Conte," *Belvedere*, II, 1927, pp. 43 ff.

118. See E. Panofsky, *Renaissance and Renascences in Western Art*, Stockholm, 1960, pp. 172–177, 200–202, and 205 for the *klassischer Idealstil* (Warburg's terminology) in figures, beginning with the sixth decade of the Quattrocento and exemplified especially in the work of Pollaiuolo, Botticelli, and Filippino Lippi. See pp. 202 and 205 for the "Neo-Gothic" precedent for "Mannerism" (both of which terms Panofsky is careful to put in quotation marks).

Warburg stressed that the antique served especially as a model for fluttering garments and hair to convey movement (A. Warburg, *Gesammelte Schriften*, Berlin, 1932, I, pp. 5 ff.). Shapley emphasized instead that there are peculiarities in the very poses and movements of Pollaiuolo's figures ("rigid exaggerated action," "affected action," "extravagance," "mannerism," "contortion," "jerkiness" were words she finds other critics and herself using) that have their prototypes in ancient vases (F. R. Shapley, "A Student of Ancient Ceramics, Antonio Pollaiuolo," *Art Bulletin*, II, 1919, pp. 78–86; cf. also A. Chastel, *Art et humanisme à Florence au temps de Laurent le Magnifique*, Paris, 1961, pp. 64 ff.). But the view prevails, nevertheless, that "the indebtedness of the Quattrocento artist to ancient art was basically one of motives rather than formal aesthetics ... Agostino di Duccio or Botticelli accept only certain ornamental devices to enhance their own expressive animation," to quote P. Bober, *Drawings after the Antique by Amico Aspertini*, pp. 20 and 22).

However, in the Botticellesque drawing after the sarcophagus in Woburn Abbey, cited by Warburg to show the relation to the antique in garments and hair (Warburg, *op. cit.*, I, p. 19, pl. IV), I think Vasari would have seen Antiquity in the angularity, the crossing arms, and the agitated two-dimensional movement, as well as in hair and drapery. These same features, of course, are basic in Botticelli's painting, together with flat lighting (cf. footnote 55 above).

The mid-Quattrocento "Gothic" current in painting (continuing from the International Gothic) would appear to have prepared for, and entered into, the employment of such features of antique art. Insofar as the term "Neo-Gothic" suggests some continuation of "Gothic" sympathies in a Botticelli or Pollaiuolo (cf. Gombrich, *Apollonio di Giovanni*, pp. 31–32) and will allow for the influence of these sympathies on the absorption of the antique, it may be a satisfactory name.

But the term helps to obscure the Neo-Gothic's significance as the first wave of Renaissance antiquizing in a characteristically Central Italian "modernly antique" vein—as one must see it, I think, when looking back from Vasari's position in the mid-Cinquecento.

(For a recent suggestion that the possible influence of the absorption of classical formal ideals on the style of Italian Renaissance art in the Quattrocento has been overlooked, see Middeldorf, *Su alcuni bronzetti all' antica del quattrocento*, pp. 67–68. Middeldorf says that classical prototypes, being largely the relief sculpture of Roman sarcophagi, easily allow themselves to be reduced to almost hieroglyphic pictorial schemes, which can give a painting or fresco an *all' antica* atmosphere. He does not go on to explore this or relate it specifically to relief-like form and movement in painting of the later Quattrocento.)

In keeping with the terminology, discussions of the "Neo-Gothic" and "Late-Gothic" precedents for "Mannerism" have not brought out the antique element. See, for example, F. Antal, "Gedanken zur Entwicklung der Trecento- und Quattrocentomalerei in Siena und Florenz," *Jahrbuch für Kunstwissenschaft*, II, 1924, pp. 219–221, 227–229, and Adelmann and Weise, *Das Fortleben gotischer Ausdrucks- und Bewegungsmotive in der Kunst des Manierismus, passim*, especially the summary and bibliography in pp. 34 ff. and related footnotes. (Elsewhere, Weise has mentioned antique twisting poses in medieval art and their contribution, via the Middle Ages, to the late Gothic of the fifteenth century: Georg Weise, "Spätgotisches Schreiten und andere Motive spätgotischer Ausdrucks- und Bewegungsstilisierung," *Marburger Jahrbuch für Kunstwissenschaft*, XIV, 1949, pp. 182–183. Yet he does not find the antique in Mannerism and puts the development of Mannerism entirely in terms of the Gothic tradition.)

Mrs. Bober, writing of Aspertini, has suggested that, besides his personal capricious fantasy, stylistic tendencies of the Quattrocento helped to prepare his attraction to, and affinity with, Antonine and Late Antonine relief, which in her view then reinforced these tendencies in his work and his own bent (see footnote 107 above and P. Bober, *op. cit.*, pp. 27–29). But if, as I assume, Roman relief and kindred antiquities had already taken stylistic effect in the main stream of "Neo-Gothic," then their influence there was available to condition the interests and development of an Aspertini from the beginning. And the same goes for the more purely "early mannerist" painters of the early Cinquecento.

119. For these and their antique models see Ernst Kris, *Meister und Meisterwerke der Steinschneidekunst in der italienischen Renaissance*, Vienna, 1929, II, pls. 5–11 and pp. 20 ff.

120. See John Pope-Hennessy, *Italian Renaissance Sculpture*, London, 1958, figs. 138–9 and pp. 101–102 and 320 for the relation of Bertoldo's relief to a specific sarcophagus at Pisa.

121. Cf. the *Virgin and Saint Anne* (in a different respect in each version), *Saint John the Baptist*, and *Leda*, as well as an angular application of his new but always motivated vocabulary and an occasional flatness in some drawings: Kenneth Clark, *Leonardo da Vinci, an Account of his Development as an Artist*, Cambridge, 1952, pls. 35, 50, 66, and 41, and A. E. Popham, *The Drawings of Leonardo da Vinci*, New York, 1945, pls. 9, 39, 48, 101, 105, 176, 212, and 213B. Consideration of the latter tendencies raises questions about Leonardo's relationship, not only to "Neo-Gothic", but to the antique. For observations on the antique and certain figures and motifs of Leonardo, see Damon T. Holcomb, *A Study of Posture and Gesture in the Figures of Leonardo da Vinci*, unpublished thesis, New York University, 1958, pp. 270–281. Holcomb plans to publish the more significant of his findings. (See also Bettina H. Polak, "A Leonardo Drawing and the Medici Gem," *Journal of the Warburg and Courtauld Institutes*, XIV, 1951, pp. 303–304.)

122. B. Berenson, *The Study and Criticism of Italian Art*, London, 1916, especially pp. 22–23, 26–27, 32. (Besides his chief points, he calls attention also to the finish of the paintings, which Vasari considered one of Leonardo's contributions.)

123. Cf. the *Annunciation*, in S. J. Freedberg, *Painting of the High Renaissance in Rome and Florence*, Cambridge, 1961, II, fig. 259.

124. See the figure at far right in the *Doni Madonna* making the unmotivated antique gesture of arm across chest (Freedberg, *High Renaissance*, II, fig. 27).

The *Battle of Cascina* (*ibid.*, fig. 36) introduced to early Cinque-cento painting, in an inescapable way, an idiom akin in figure and composition to the Roman sculptured relief style that Bertoldo's *Battle* had presented earlier in sculpture. Michelangelo thus brought back with a vengeance into painting the influence of a relief concept, present in rather different form in "Neo-Gothic" painting (cf. Pol-laiuolo's *Martyrdom of Saint Sebastian*), and put it into deadly conflict with the pure High Renaissance idiom of flowing harmony and pliant figures in unity with space, at a moment when there had scarcely been time for the High Renaissance to take hold. The nature of the relief concept is underlined by comparing the *Battle of Cascina* both with detailed photographs of Bertoldo's relief (see Pope-Hennessy, *Italian Renaissance Sculpture*, pls. 92–93) and with the Gigantomachy on a sarcophagus in the Vatican (my Figure 16), a work not known in the Renaissance, to be sure.

In the years after the *Battle of Cascina*, influences from Roman relief, of various kinds, counter the pure High Renaissance increas-ingly. Near the end of this essay I suggest that the forces that made the High Renaissance yield the field stem above all from these influences.

125. Cf. J. Wilde, *Italian Drawings in the Department of Prints and Drawings in the British Museum, Michelangelo and his Studio*, London, 1953, pls. XXIX, XXX and pp. 29–31. For Sebastiano's *Resurrection of Lazarus*, see Freedberg, II, pl. 463.

126. Cf. the fourth figure from the right on the sarcophagus with the Fall of Phaeton in the Uffizi, Florence, the sarcophagus that prob-ably was the iconographic source for Michelangelo's drawings of the legend of Phaeton; Charles de Tolnay, *Michelangelo*, III, *The Medici Chapel*, Princeton, 1948, fig. 294. The points of correspond-ence include the legs, difficult to see in the reproduction. I am grateful to Mrs. Grippi for this derivation, which will be included in her publication.

127. Freedberg, II, fig. 200.
For an awareness of the way the general aspect of the *Raising of Lazarus* anticipates future painting, see De Tolnay, *The Medici Chapel*, p. 18, where, however, German and Netherlandish influences are held responsible instead of Roman relief, as I would have it.

128. Cf. H. Wölfflin, *Classic Art,* London, 1952, p. 99; Freedberg, II, fig. 160.

129. For specific relationships to the antique, see E. Panofsky, *Renaissance and Renascences in Western Art,* pp. 202–203, including the reference to Winternitz.

130. The vein of *dolcezza* as Dolce defined it in contrast to that which he called "pieno di muscoli": see Barocchi, *Trattati d'arte,* I, pp. 177 to 178. The distinction between the muscled and delicate ways of doing the nude is found earlier in Leonardo (*ibid.,* p. 465, note 6), who argued against the muscled on scientific grounds rather than Dolce's aesthetic ones, and it must go right on into *maniera* painting. One vein does not really belong more fully to *maniera* than the other, if one accepts the bases of *maniera* given in this paper. And both are clearly in evidence (cf. the distinction of this sort that Weisbach observed in mannerist painting; *Der Manierismus,* pp. 165 ff.). As Dolce said, the weight of antique precedence was for *dolcezza* (Barocchi, *op. cit.,* I, pp. 178 and 195)—although the antique gave full precedence for muscled figures as well. On the other hand, Dolce thought some painters took refuge in *dolcezza* because they were incapable of handling muscles correctly and hence executed figures by doing only the principal contours. Here he touches on the characteristic of *maniera* draftsmanship that Van Mander called convenient and cursory (see footnotes 63 and 64 above). For several versions of the same subject, now inclining more to muscles, now more to *dolcezza,* see Vasari's drawings and paintings of the *Immaculate Conception* (Figs. 2a, 2b, 25, 26).

131. F. Hartt, "Raphael and Giulio Romano," *Art Bulletin,* XXVI, 1944, p. 72; Freedberg, II, fig. 374.

132. Cf. my *Bronzino Studies, op. cit.,* p. 246. The Borghese *Entombment* exemplifies the beginning of this Roman relief trend in Raphael and his circle (see Arnold von Salis, *Antike und Renaissance,* Zurich, 1947, pp. 61 ff. for the painting's relation to the antique, and footnote 8 above) and the *Battle of Constantine* its continuation after the *Ostia* (see Von Salis, pp. 74 ff.). For another aspect of the trend, see the prominent example of the Louvre *Saint Michael* (Freedberg, II, fig. 437).

If to our eyes such works flawed the classic style of the High Renaissance, which we place highest, we have to remember that they had nevertheless a Renaissance justification and the trend they represented won the day.

For anticipations of *maniera* tendencies in color in Raphael and his following, see Harry Manz, *Die Farbgebung in der italienischen Malerei des Protobarock und Manierismus*, Munich, 1934, pp. 63–68. (Michelangelo's color and something of its relation to the color of *maniera* paintings are also discussed: see especially pp. 51–54. For this see also the more recent treatment in Charles de Tolnay, *Michelangelo*, II, *The Sistine Ceiling*, Princeton, 1945, pp. 99–101.)

133. For anticipations of *maniera* in Giulio's use of antique poses, see again the paper by Gombrich, "The Style *all' antica:* Imitation and Assimilation," *Acts of the XXth International Congress, op. cit.*

By the time of the Sala di Troia, Giulio's work, too, tends to take on the appearance of *maniera*, as Kugler saw: see footnote 8 above. Cf. also nineteenth century opinions on Giulio and antiquity in footnote 8.

134. Bernice F. Davidson, *Marcantonio Raimondi, the Engravings of the Roman Period*, dissertation for Harvard University, 1954, pp. 30, 34, 42–49, 55–58, 63–64, 66, 95, 105, explains the exclusion of irregularity in Marcantonio's prints as due to the influence of ancient sculpture. She mentions various aspects of his work that anticipate *maniera*.

Armenini thought the study of prints led to crudeness (*De' veri precetti*, p. 5).

135. See, for example, the illustrations of Aspertini's sketchbooks in P. Bober, *Drawings after the Antique by Amico Aspertini*. One would never confuse Aspertini's earlier drawings after the antique with *maniera* works or even with a *maniera* artist's drawings after the antique. But Aspertini's latest drawings show differences from the early ones that reflect, I should say, the contemporary intensification of the conventions of the figure into *maniera*.

136. *Ibid.*, pp. 24–26.

137. L. Becherucci, *Manieristi toscani*, Bergamo, 1944, pl. 40.

138. *Ibid.*, pls. 46 and 135.

139. *Ibid.*, pl. 10. Under the influence probably of the impact of antique relief on painters in Rome (Gamba, *Contributo alla conoscenza del Pontormo*, Florence, 1956, p. 9, has suggested a trip to Rome before the Visdomini altarpiece)—this with his left hand, while with his right he did something quite different a little later at Poggio a Caiano, to borrow Frank Lloyd Wright's comment on two currents of about the same time in his own architecture.

140. Freedberg, *High Renaissance*, II, figs. 194, 195. Related to, but more monumental than, what Freedberg calls the archaeological style (cf. fig. 179), Sodoma's work, like the *maniera* of the future, is not literally *all' antica*.

141. Compare Freedberg, II, fig. 494 and Krautheimer with Krautheimer-Hess, *Lorenzo Ghiberti*, fig. 137. Mrs. Grippi has chosen this comparison as the closest.

142. Freedberg, II, fig. 487.
Peruzzi was capable of widely differing modes for different purposes at more or less the same moment, as was Perino. Such versatility in style begins to be a phenomenon to reckon with in painting by the second decade of the century and more so in the third. The importance of Peruzzi's *Presentation* for "early Mannerism" has been stressed (see F. Antal, "Observations on Girolamo da Carpi," *Art Bulletin*, XXX, 1948, p. 85, footnote 25 and, recently, Freedberg, I, pp. 410–411). But the *Presentation*, the *Heracles*, and — more strictly *all' antica* — the *Quos Ego* (Freedberg, II, fig. 486, tentatively attributed there to Peruzzi) all anticipate something of *maniera*, each in its own way.

143. Becherucci, *Manieristi toscani*, pls. 103–105.

144. Cf. Henri Delaborde, *Marc-Antoine Raimondi, étude critique et historique suivie d'un catalogue raisonné des œuvres du maître*, Paris, 1888, illustration p. 53.
Armenini recommended Bandinelli's work along with Michelangelo's as proper for the young painter's study, following work

after the antique (*De' veri precetti*, p. 62). His influence on Salviati is discussed in Cheney, *Francesco Salviati (1510–1563)*. For his "Raphaelesque moment," relevant in the present connection, see L. Marcucci, "Disegni del Bandinelli per la Strage degli innocenti," *Rivista d'arte*, series 3, IV, 1954, p. 106.

145. See Rolf Kultzen, "Die Malerei Polidoros da Caravaggio im Giardino del Bufalo in Rom," *Mitteilungen des Kunsthistorischen Instituts in Florenz*, IX, 1959–1960, figs. 4–11, 13–18 and pp. 109 and 112. The same is true of the light. But see fig. 20 and p. 111 for the way in which on occasion he anticipated *maniera* rather more.

146. Vasari-Milanesi, V, pp. 143–144 and IV, p. 13.

147. See C. Gamba, "Un disegno e un chiaroscuro di Pierin del Vaga," *Rivista d'arte*, V, 1907, pp. 91–92 and A. E. Popham, "On Some Works by Perino del Vaga," *Burlington Magazine*, LXXXVI, 1945, pp. 64–65.

148. See, for example, S. J. Freedberg, *Parmigianino, His Works in Painting*, Cambridge, 1950, pls. 21–23.

149. *Ibid.*, pls. 57, 64, 65.

150. F. Hartt, review of P. Barocchi's *Rosso Fiorentino*, *Art Bulletin*, XXXIV, 1952, p. 68. For this in Bronzino, see Smyth, *The Earliest Works of Bronzino*, pp. 202–205.

151. Becherucci, *Manieristi toscani*, pl. 74; also the *Rebecca and Eliezar*, copied by Salviati (cf. F. Antal in *Old Master Drawings*, XIV, 1939–1940, pl. 44, and the catalogue, *Mostra del Pontormo e del primo manierismo fiorentino*, 2nd ed., Florence, 1956, pl. CIV).

152. Becherucci, *op. cit.*, pl. 79. I am grateful to Eugene Carroll for assuring me that this is the earliest instance in Rosso's work.

153. Cf. Sebastiano's drawing in Chatsworth of one of the apostles of the *Transfiguration* in San Pietro in Montorio (R. Pallucchini, *Sebastian Viniziano*, Milan, 1944, pl. 97). I find that Bronzino must, almost certainly, have met Sebastiano personally at Pesaro. For

the evidence for this and for Bronzino's work at Pesaro, see my book on the decorations of the Villa Imperiale, which I hope will be ready shortly for publication. The basis for attributing the two works mentioned in this paper and others at Pesaro is presented there. The photograph used for Fig. 23 shows nineteenth century retouching, which was being removed in 1962. The figure illustrated in Fig. 22 is not significantly retouched.

154. At the opening of the 1530's Michelangelo, Bandinelli, Pontormo, and Bronzino were the main artists in Florence. All helped to promote the *maniera* idiom. Pontormo did so after 1530 under the direct influence of Michelangelo, Bronzino under the same influence surely, but also under Rosso's, Sebastiano's, and the Raphael School's, all of which he felt at Pesaro. His work there, so early in the 'thirties, suggests that he contributed toward the development of the conventions of pose and light and also of *maniera* contour, sculpturesqueness, uniform substance, classicizing faces, and impersonal expressions. Even without knowing his share in the Pesaro decorations, Voss, *Die Malerei der Spätrenaissance*, I, p. 210, believed that he took "the decisive step to the Mannerism of Vasari and his followers." It is worth putting on record in this connection that Vasari worked as Bronzino's assistant on one occasion in 1533: see A. del Vita, *Il libro delle ricordanze di Giorgio Vasari*, p. 20.

155. J. Wilde, "Notes on the Genesis of Michelangelo's *Leda*," in *Fritz Saxl, 1890–1948, a Volume of Memorial Essays from his Friends in England*, ed. D. J. Gordon, London, 1957, especially pp. 279–280; also *idem*, "Michelangelo and Leonardo," *Burlington Magazine*, XCV, 1953, p. 77.

156. See footnote 126 above and De Tolnay, *The Medici Chapel*, figs. 151–153, 294 and *idem*, *Michelangelo*, V, *The Final Period*, Princeton, 1960, fig. 131.

157. Salviati's copy of Michelangelo's *Phaeton* (Vasari-Milanesi, VII, p. 17), Battista Franco's use of the *Dream* and *Ganymede* in the *Battle of Montemurlo* (A. Venturi, *Storia dell' arte italiana*, IX, 6, Milan, 1933, fig. 156), Pontormo's adaptations (discussed in Janet Cox Rearick's forthcoming book on Pontormo's drawings), as well as

the influence on Michael Coxie's drawings of the *Loves of Jupiter* in the British Museum (treated by Mary Stone, *Michael Coxie in Rome, with an Appendix on his Later Career and a Handlist of his Works*, unpublished master's thesis, New York University, 1957), and the copy of the *Ganymede* by Daniele da Volterra (cf. M. L. Mez, *Daniele da Volterra*, dissertation, Hamburg, 1932, p. 60). In March, 1532 Sebastiano del Piombo asked Michelangelo for a sketch for the "invenzione" of the Chigi altarpiece in S. Maria del Popolo, but it is not known that he received or used it (see De Tolnay, *The Medici Chapel*, p. 21).

Precisely from the close of the crucial decade in the development of *maniera* comes Aretino's praise of Salviati's draftsmanship in connection with its debt to Michelangelo: see the letter to Leone Leoni of July 11, 1539 in Pertile and Camesca, *Lettere sull' arte di Pietro Aretino, op. cit.*, I, pp. 130–131. (I owe my knowledge of this letter to Iris H. Cheney).

Great as is the appreciation of Michelangelo's influence on "mature Mannerism," the tendency has been to think less in terms of the drawings he did around 1530 in Florence or the *Leda* than of the sculptures of the Medici Tombs and the *Last Judgment*, although the latter was not finished until the 'thirties were over. (For example, Dvořák, *Geschichte der italienischen Kunst*, II, pp. 127 ff.) Later, to be sure, the *Last Judgment* became the main work by Michelangelo for study (Armenini recommends it to the young painter immediately after study from the antique, *De' veri precetti*, p. 58).

Perhaps Michelangelo's style in drawing and painting of around 1530 was itself stimulated by such other developments toward *maniera* conventions as we have noted, developments which he himself helped to instigate from an early time.

For the enormous regard in which Michelangelo's contemporaries held him and for expressions of their views on his relation to the antique, see E. Battisti, "La critica a Michelangelo prima del Vasari," *Rinascimento*, V, 1954, pp. 115 ff.

158. Such as some of those stressed by Weisbach, *Der Manierismus*, pp. 166 ff. or Blunt, *Artistic Theory in Italy*, p. 86.

159. For a recent view of the Mannerists' transformation of poses as stressing elegance, see James Holderbaum, "Notes on Tribolo-I:

a Documented Bronze by Tribolo," *Burlington Magazine*, XCIX, 1957, pp. 336 ff.

160. Cf. Adelmann and Weise, *Das Fortleben gotischer Ausdrucks- und Bewegungsmotive in der Kunst des Manierismus*, pp. 26 ff. for the exaggeration of contrasting directions in several axes.

161. Ragghianti had a certain view of this when he called San Giovanni Decollato a center "di Michelangiolismo riformato e antichizzato, 'bronzinesco,'" where "Michelangelism became tempered with Raphaelism and Emilian tendencies—an impassioned stylization." See C. L. Ragghianti, review of Fiocco's "L'Eredità di Giovanni Demio," *La Critica d' Arte*, IV–V, nos. 3–4, 1939–1940, pt. 2, pp. iv–v.

162. The extraordinarily energetic steps taken to transform the route of Charles V's triumphal entry into Rome in 1536 (see R. Lanciani, *The Golden Days of the Renaissance in Rome from the Pontificate of Julius II to that of Paul III*, Boston-New York, 1906, pp. 101, 110–111) suggest a wave of enthusiasm for reinstating Rome's ancient glory in decorative splendor. It seems likely to have been the lost decorations for this occasion that constituted the main event for the development of *maniera* in the 'thirties; for they must have offered the opportunity to demonstrate the possibilities of modernized antique idiom on a grand scale.

163. Vasari-Milanesi, IV, p. 9.
    L. Venturi, *La Critica di Giorgio Vasari*, pp. 32–36, considers that *regola* refers only to architecture here. Although he points out that *licenzia*, when applied to architecture, means license within the rules for using the ancient orders (cf. Vasari-Milanesi, VII, p. 193; also I, p. 135–136), he believes that, applied to painting, it means license with respect to nature (an interpretation coinciding with the concept of Mannerism as deliberate deviation from nature). (See also the interpretation by Rosci, *Manierismo e accademismo*, pp. 66–67.) Milanesi remarks that Vasari applies *regola* and the other four terms of the *proemio* in Book III to painting and sculpture, though in the beginning they pertain only to architecture. (Cf. Vasari-Milanesi, IV, p. 7, note 1). The context, starting with the mention of Giotto

(p. 8), makes the reference to painting clear. For another recent interpretation of the passage, cf. Paola Barocchi, "Il valore dell' antico nella storiografia vasariana," *Convegno internazionale sul rinascimento*, V, Florence, 1956, pp. 228 ff.

164. Milanesi (Vasari-Milanesi, IV, p. 7, note 1), commenting on the obscurity of Vasari's terms, remarks that *regola* was used in medieval architecture to signify the fundamental form according to which the parts were constructed and their relations established and that afterwards it was used exclusively by the Italians in relation to Roman architecture, when, with Brunelleschi and Alberti, they began to imitate it. The definition of *regola* in *maniera* painting might, I am tempted to think, run similarly: the fundamental form, derived ultimately from the antique, according to which the parts were constructed and their relations established. (As I understand him, rather the same opinion may be held by Rouchette, *La renaissance que nous a léguée Vasari*, p. 100 and pp. 89–90.)

The following uses do not seem out of keeping with such a definition. Armenini (*De' veri precetti*, p. 61) believed that, when a painter formed a *bella maniera* by continually copying the antique, his works were "done well through a certain *regola*." Apropos of Vasari's remarks on Titian's late works, Agostino Carracci wrote: "In questa parte, e nelle altre anco, ma perchè non si servirono delle odiose regole dei pittori fiorentini, il Vasari le dà del crosta..." (See A. del Vita, "L'Animosità di Agostino Carracci contro il Vasari," *Il Vasari*, 1958, p. 65.) *Regole* here seems to make good sense if taken as a reflection of the *maniera* artist's use of *regola* with the meaning I suggest. To Vincenzo Danti (Barocchi, *Trattati d'arte*, I, pp. 211 to 212), *regola* together with *ordine* was something "che si può o dee osservare intorno alla perfetta composizione delle parti de' membri, che al loro tutto della figura umana si convengono," but he said he had learned it from Michelangelo. Cf. also Paolo Pino, *Dialogo di pittura* in Barocchi, *op. cit.*, I, p. 106.

165. Comparable, that is, to Vasari's use of *licenzia* in relation to architecture; see footnote 163. It pertains to modernizing the antique.

166. Vasari-Milanesi, I, pp. 169–170; 174–175; VII, p. 427.

Some of the various modes in Cinquecento drawing may, it seems to me, have been inspired by the varied modes of handling in antique relief; compare Figs. 11 and 17, 12 and 14.

167. See Barocchi, *Trattati d'arte*, I, p. 179.

168. For the value Vasari placed on "furore artistico" see Vasari-Milanesi, II, p. 171; E. H. Gombrich, *Art and Illusion*, pp. 188–189, 192–195; L. Venturi, *La critica di Giorgio Vasari*, pp. 37–38; Luigi Grassi, "I concetti di schizzo, abbozzo, macchia, 'non-finito,' e la costruzione dell' opera d'arte," *Studi in onore di Pietro Silva*, Florence, 1955, pp. 97 ff.; Francesco Flora, "Giorgio Vasari scrittore e storico delle arti," *Il Vasari,* n. s. 15, 1957, p. 10; Paola Barocchi, "Finito e non-finito nella critica vasariana," *Arte antica e moderna*, No. 3, July-Sept., 1958, pp. 221 ff.

For the change in the concept of *disegno* during the Cinquecento, coinciding with the drawing's importance as the arena for invention versus painting as its exterior, technical realization, see Panofsky, *Idea*, p. 45 and note 194. Compare the Florentine's definition of *invenzione* in Pino, *Dialogo di pittura* (Barocchi, *Trattati d'arte*, p. 115). For Leonardo's contribution to this aspect of drawing through his concept and use of the free sketch, see E. H. Gombrich, *op. cit.*, and *idem,* "Conseils de Léonard sur les esquisses de tableau," *L'Art et la pensée de Léonard de Vinci, Communications du Congrès international du Val de Loire* (July, 1952), *Etudes d'art*, nos. 8–10, Paris-Alger, 1953–1954, pp. 179–197. For a passage suggesting that Vasari recognized something of Leonardo's contribution in drawing, see his introduction to Part III of the *Lives*, mentioned above, p. 13.

See also Armenini's pertinent remarks on the function of the quick sketch cited in footnote 69 above.

169. Uffizi no. 705F is a study for Naldini's *Adoration of the Christ Child* in Santa Maria Novella (Venturi, *Storia dell' arte italiana*, IX, part 5, fig. 145). Uffizi no. 9011S is a study for his lunette of the *Presentation* in San Pierino (*ibid.*, fig. 147).

170. See Vasari-Milanesi, I, pp. 169, 171 (where *pratica* is connected particularly with drawing), 172, 173, and VII, p. 427 (cf. footnote 38 above). See also *Lezzione di Benedetto Varchi, nella quale si disputa della*

maggioranza delle arti... l'anno 1546, Florence, 1549, as reprinted in Barocchi, *Trattati d'arte*, I, pp. 31–32; and Pino, *Dialogo di pittura*, in Barocchi, *op. cit.*, I, pp. 117–118, 113–114. (Lomazzo later says *pratica* is the *ragione* with which the painter composes; Lomazzo, *Trattato dell' arte de la pittura*, Milan, 1584, p. 281.)

Cf. Armenini's admiring description of Giulio Romano's copiousness and ease in composing out of his head in his drawings, thanks to "la sua maniera tanto conforme, e prossimana alle scolture antiche di Roma, che per esser vi stato studiosissimo sempre mentre era giovane, che ciò che deponeva, e formava pareva esser proprio cavato da quelle" (Armenini, *De' veri precetti*, p. 76).

171. They were "making" more than "matching," to use Gombrich's terms (*Art and Illusion*, pp. 186–187), in accord with their strong "mental set."

172. See many illustrations in the catalogue *Le triomphe du manièrisme européen de Michel-ange au Gréco*, Rijksmuseum, Amsterdam, 1955.

173. The conventions of space lent themselves to cultivating the abrupt and the unexpected, particularly with respect to its extent and to relationships between divisions. It is here that *licenzia* seems to have played its chief part spatially.

174. This is partly what Venetian painters did when they employed *maniera* more in terms of flesh and blood and the painted surface than of sculpture and gave it, in the realm of painting, some of the advantages of the free sketch in drawing. *Maniera* responded by stimulating Venetian painting both decoratively and expressively, as Titian's mythologies of the 'fifties or his *Saint Lawrence* of the 'sixties bear witness. (Cf. the view that Mannerism furnished Venetian painting the means of escaping naturalism, in L. Coletti, "La crisi manieristica nella pittura veneziana," *Convivium*, XIII, 1941, pp. 109–126, but see also G. N. Fasola, "Il manierismo e l'arte veneziana del cinquecento," *Atti del XVIII Congresso internazionale di storia dell' arte*, 1955, Venice, pp. 291–293.)

175. Zeri, *Pittura e controriforma*, is helpful in showing several masters of this sort.

The question whether Michelangelo should be called a Mannerist has become difficult to approach objectively. (See, however, note 36 above.) But this question aside, he put features of *maniera* to marvelous use. The flattened poses, flat light, and jarring dissonances of juxtaposition and angularity in the *Conversion of Saint Paul* embody the cataclysmic effect of the apparition on the saint and on the soldiers dispersing in terror.

176. See footnote 88.

177. Mannerism as preparation for the Baroque was emphasized early in twentieth century criticism. See, for example, M. Hoerner, cited in footnote 196 below.

178. For Rubens' *De imitazione statuarum*, see Gaeler von Ravensburg, *Rubens und die Antike*, Jena, 1882, pp. 195–196 (and p. 37, a German translation from the Latin). Rubens warned painters that they must use sculptural models with insight and not "let the stone leave its stamp," that the experienced as well as inexperienced "do not differentiate the material from the form, the stone from the human figure, and the compulsion of the marble *(necessitatem marmoris)* from art." To work as a beginner from sculptural models makes one's painting "crude, circumscribed, and difficult," and it is bad for anatomy. The results are "to the dishonor of nature" and like "marble rather than flesh, in coloring." Sculpture is an influence for undifferentiated, abrupt shading, for modeling that does not suggest the subtle variety and pliableness of the skin as the body moves, for lighted surfaces that "lift up and are even [the Latin is *par*; does he mean "flat"?] or at least blinding to the eyes." Rubens' comments were cited by Goldschmidt, *Lambert Lombard*, p. 206, in relation to sixteenth century Netherlandish painting. Clearly the example of *maniera* painting in Italy as well as in the Lowlands was in Rubens' mind.

Armenini also saw dangers in copying antique sculpture, as well as sculptural models by Bandinelli or Michelangelo (*De' veri precetti*, pp. 5, 87–88).

179. The sudden, surprising appearance of somewhat crude execution in the Raphael circle at Rome, in work done in Raphael's

name (as in the *Stanza dell' Incendio*) and just after his death (the *Sala di Costantino*), coincides with this circle's intense new study of antiquities. Is it not possible that sheer saturation in antique figures and reliefs, the majority of which were crude by prevailing standards in painting, had to do with this phenomenon and with making it acceptable? (Cf., however, recently, Coffin, *Villa d'Este*, p. 76.)

180. Thus weakening the ornamental integrity of the picture surface. In the interstices between volumes there are apt to be holes without positive value in the surface. Volumes themselves tend to be too insistently sculpturesque to belong to the surface, seeming simply to exist behind it or to be so far forward as to interrupt it, to be in the very place of it and effective in disintegrating it.

181. In this connection we may recall the practice of studying individual figures and compositions from small sculptured models, which was in keeping with the sculpturesque ideal (see Vasari-Milanesi, I, p. 170 and Armenini, *De' veri precetti*, pp. 93–94, 97).
   The continual use and re-use of the same models (*ibid.*, p. 67) and the use, by some painters, of a few adjustable models, adjustable for the purpose of studying any figure in any pose, is curiously suitable to Vasari's ideal of one figure for all figures (*ibid.*, pp. 98–99.)

182. Described well by Armenini, *ibid.*, pp. 70–71, who thought elaborate invention, at too great speed, more appropriate to temporary decorations than to dignified, permanent works. Perhaps influence tended to spread from the former to the latter. Do the decorations of San Giovanni Decollato reflect stylistic developments in the lost decorations for the entry of Charles V?

183. From the Cinquecento to the present it has been axiomatic that speed bore a large responsibility for lack of quality in mid- and later sixteenth century painting. In view of the other factors that we see working against quality and of what we know today about the achievements of speed in some other artistic contexts, was it really speed by itself that was so injurious?

184. Cf. Voss, *Die Malerei der Spätrenaissance*, II, p. 337.

185. An aesthetic for all: cf. Joseph Meder, *Die Handzeichnung, ihre Technik und Entwicklung*, Vienna, 1923, p. 20.

186. Yet one cannot disregard the weight of great works of the past, which both nineteenth and twentieth century critics have emphasized. They must have created "pressure" on the artist and have held for him always some danger of his "being dazzled by genius." (Cf. *The Writer's Dilemma*, London, Oxford University Press, 1961, p. 41.)

187. See footnote 6 above.

188. Cf. footnote 130 above.

189. Although nineteenth century critics lacked sympathy with the result and did not see the role of antique relief, they partly grasped this (cf. Burckhardt's observation that Mannerism may have started with the superficial application of forms and methods of expression begun by the greatest masters as something conventionally ideal; quoted in W. Weisbach, *Manierismus in mittelalterlicher Kunst*, Basel, 1942, p. 9).

190. Gombrich's results in *Art and Illusion* help us to see that, while *maniera* can be laid to a conscious purpose, its development must have involved also a yielding to the patterns that artists had learned to handle from the study of what most preoccupied them (see especially pp. 25, 77–90, 64, 156, 293, 394). As the concept of uncomprehending imitation recedes, this concept must take part of its place.

191. An interlude in the Central Italian development of a modernized antique style beginning in the Quattrocento (cf. footnote 118 above), an interlude owing to the temporary dominance of classic harmonious naturalness, also with precedents in antiquity.

It is not satisfactory to trace the history of Italian painting simply in terms of a swing back and forth between opposites, but one can see here two tendencies that were conflicting (like the Late Gothic and classic, or "classicist," that Antal stressed), one stemming from Roman relief, the other from the striving for the ideally natural, in keeping with the classic aspect of classical art. In view of the overriding interest of critics, until well into our century, in the Renaissance conquest of nature and its outcome in the High Renaissance, it was to be expected that the somewhat contrary effect on painting exerted by the Renaissance preoccupation with antique relief should not be taken into full account. Awareness of the role of Roman relief in representing antiquity to the Renaissance painter helps us, I think, to understand better such phenomena as the dissociation of figures and space in Florentine painting of the later Quattrocento, its emphasis on limbs (cf. footnote 56 above), and its light (cf. footnote 55). And it illuminates tendencies right in the midst of High Renaissance painting that conflict, to our eyes, with pure High Renaissance style (cf. footnote 124).

192. The conviction that, in literature, the later Cinquecento does not reject the Renaissance but elaborates it, developing a new sensibility and taste, has been expressed recently by Riccardo Scrivano, *Il manierismo nella letteratura del cinquecento*, especially pp. 21, 26.

193. Cf., for example, Meder, *Die Handzeichnung*, pp. 17 ff. (earlier, Fiorillo, *Geschichte der Mahlerei*, I, pp. 152 ff.).

194. Recently, for example, E. Berti Toesca, "Mostra del Pontormo e del primo manierismo fiorentino," *Bollettino d'arte*, XLI, 1956, pp. 280–282.

195. Applied to literature by E. R. Curtius, *European Literature and the Latin Middle Ages*, New York, 1953, pp. 274, 282 ff., 292 ff. (see also footnote 201 below). Cf. earlier, for example, H. Grimm, *Leben Michelangelos*, 5th ed., Berlin, 1879, I, p. 491.
   The relation Curtius sees between Spanish Mannerism, in particular, and the rhetorical tradition in Latin writing of the late Roman Empire bears a similarity to the relation between *maniera* painting and Roman relief style, even to the Spanish modernization of the antique system of rhetoric by means of the novelty and brilliance of modern conceits; Curtius, pp. 291, 295–300. (It is suggestive to contemplate the relation he indicates between "Latin Mannerism of Late Antiquity," rhetoric in the Middle Ages, and Spanish literary Mannerism of the seventeenth century.)

196. See M. Hoerner, "Manierismus," *Zeitschrift für Ästhetik und all-gemeine Kunstwissenschaft*, XVII, 1923/24, pp. 262–268, where Mannerism is a recurring stage in the evolution of styles from classic to baroque.

197. Standard dictionary usage. Cf. also, for example, Curtius, *op. cit.*, p. 282.

198. Mannerism is implied in Focillon's "age of refinement," the third of four ages or states through which forms pass "at every epoch and in every environment," the others being the experimental age, the classic age, and the baroque age: Henri Focillon, *The Life of Forms in Art*, 2nd ed., New York, 1948, pp. 10 ff.

199. And the emptiness and meaninglessness suggested by several of the concepts obscure the classicizing and idealizing significance that *maniera* conventions must have had for the Cinquecento artist.

All these views of Mannerism survive or develop from the nineteenth century (cf. footnote 8 above).

200. For stress on grace, see Fröhlich-Bum, *Parmigianino und der Manierismus*, p. 119 (she sees Mannerism as deriving chiefly from Parmigianino). Cf. John Shearman, "*Maniera* as an Aesthetic Ideal," *Acts of the XXth International Congress of the History of Art, Studies of Western Art*, Princeton University Press, forthcoming, volume II. (I heard this paper but have not read it.) For emphasis on elegance, see, for example, K. Clark, *The Nude*, pp. 135–139, and the implied concept of Mannerism in Weise's two articles (cited in footnote 31 above).

201. It would be wide of the fundamentals of *maniera* to make the erotic element, often though it occurs in *maniera*, central to Mannerism, as it sometimes threatens to become.

202. On the contrary, the role of conformity is considerable in *maniera*, conformity to the conventions of the "modernly antique."

203. See Hocke, *Die Welt als Labyrinth*, pp. 225–226. Hocke's formulation was influenced, as he says, by the ideas of Curtius.

In applying the term Mannerism to literature, Curtius preferred a broadened meaning, which seems to stem partly from the concept of Mannerism as deviation from the classic norm of the High Renaissance and partly from his view of Mannerism as elaboration in which form is not naturally suited to the subject (footnote 195 above). He wants to free Mannerism from all art-historical connotations and have it represent "simply the common denominator for all literary tendencies which are opposed to Classicism, whether they be pre-classical, post-classical, or contemporary with any Classicism. Understood in this sense, Mannerism is a constant in European literature. It is the complementary phenomenon of the Classicism of all periods. The polarity of Classicism and Mannerism is...a conceptual instrument." For this he finds Mannerism preferable to the word "Baroque." (Curtius, *European Literature and the Latin Middle Ages*, pp. 273, 291). But rebellion and expressionism are not part of Curtius' common denominator.

For a striking example of transferring the term Mannerism in the sense chiefly of abnormality (related to the concept of deviation from the classic norm) to another period and art, see its use for "crazy" medieval rib vaults by P. Frankl, "The Crazy Vaults of Lincoln Cathedral," *Art Bulletin*, XXXV, 1953, pp. 104–106.

204. E. H. Gombrich, "Zum Werke Giulio Romanos," *Jahrbuch der kunsthistorischen Sammlungen in Wien*, N. F. IX, 1935, pp. 140 ff.; *idem, The Story of Art*, London, 1950, pp. 265–266; *idem*, review of A. Hauser, *Social History of Art* in *Art Bulletin*, XXXV, 1953, p. 82; *idem*, "The Renaissance Concept of Artistic Progress and its Consequences," *Actes du XVIIme Congrès international d'histoire de l'art*, Amsterdam, *1952*, The Hague, 1955, pp. 293–294, 301; *idem, Raphael's* "*Madonna della Sedia*," London, 1956, p. 24; *idem, Art and Illusion*, pp. 20–21.

See also Mario Salmi, "La mostra del cinquecento toscano," *Nuova antologia*, LXXV, no. 410, July-August, 1940, pp. 75 ff., for the observation that Mannerism should not be traced to social and religious movements.

Recently Longhi has stated his conception of early Mannerism as a matter of individual originality, an artistic matter, not explainable by events and calamities and not essentially anticlassic or anti-Renaissance: R. Longhi, "Ricordo dei manieristi," *L'Approdo*, II, 1953, pp. 55 ff. Cf. also aspects of Berenson's opinion in footnote 17 above.

205. Nor was Donatello, on whom Pontormo based his *Christ before Pilate* (Fig. 1); see I. Lavin, "An Observation on 'Medievalism' in Early Sixteenth Century Style," *Gazette des Beaux-Arts*, 6th series, L, 1958, pp. 113–118. E. H. Gombrich observed in a letter concerning the present paper: then "where is it [i.e., Pontormo's picture] anticlassical?' '*H Δwvatos Bovappwtiçeι*' etc." (Cf. Vasari-Milanesi, II, p. 426.) This is the kind of question our terminology must provoke. See footnote 209 below.

As for the recourse to German sources, I think we should ask whether this was not ancillary to an urge inspired especially by antique relief and Michelangelo to engage in experiments outside the vein of ideal naturalness.

206. If the influence of Roman relief sculpture was fundamental to the unclassic style of "Neo-Gothic," as I have suggested (cf. footnote 118 above), if slightly later this influence was also at the root of the tendencies that conflicted with the High Renaissance and displaced it (cf. footnotes 124, 132, and 191 above, as well as 207 and 209 below), and if thereafter it was the basis of *maniera*, as proposed in the present essay, then the dominant trend in Renaissance painting in Florence and Rome from the mid-fifteenth century on was toward principles of Roman relief. The trend had a long development through various phases. One may be tempted to ask which we should consider the more central to Renaissance painting in Florence and Rome, this relief tradition or the classic, harmonious, ideal naturalness of the brief High Renaissance. The High Renaissance affected all Cinquecento painting fundamentally. There is no question about the radical differences between painting before and after. It also was the beginning of major painterly developments of the Baroque, as Theodor Hetzer was always at such pains to emphasize. But in the sixteenth century the relief concept of painting, based on Roman relief, stood against it in Central Italy. Although the influence of this concept intruded into the painting of Venice and of Correggio, the High Renaissance flourished longer in both and its potentialities developed further. When Venetian painting and Correggio later became the prime sources of inspiration for the anti-mannerist reaction that led to the Baroque, the reaction was against the conventions deriving largely from antique relief that had held sway in the Cinquecento. (As to Hetzer's

views on the High Renaissance and the Baroque, see his typically sweeping but illuminating and provocative generalizations in, for example, Theodor Hetzer, *Das deutsche Element in der italienischen Malerei des sechzehnten Jahrhunderts*, Berlin, 1929, pp. 145 ff.; *idem*, *Tizian, Geschichte seiner Farbe*, Frankfurt, 1944, pp. 42–56, originally published in 1935; and *idem*, "Vom Plastischen in der Malerei" originally published in 1938, in *Aufsätze und Vorträge*, Leipzig, 1957, pp. 150–153, 159. In the essay Hetzer writes in general terms of the relationship of High Renaissance painting to antique sculpture, but he has in mind the classic aspects of ancient sculpture, which are relevant to the High Renaissance.) The way in which the High Renaissance originally developed counter to the relief tradition is worth considering further, and I want to return to it elsewhere.

207. For an illustration of the whole, see Krautheimer with Krautheimer-Hess, *Lorenzo Ghiberti*, fig. 113.

For the trend of "expressionism" in Roman art beginning in the Severan Age, see Doro Levi, "L'Arte romana, schizzo della sua evoluzione e sua posizione nella storia dell' arte antica," *Annuario della Scuola archeologica italiana di Atene*, n. s. VI–X, 1944–50, Rome, 1950, pp. 265–266. Levi's characterization of the trend reads rather like a modern description of early Cinquecento post-classic painting in Tuscany.

For observations on the "correspondence . . . in the approach to the expression of emotions and spiritual activity" between Mannerism (meaning especially early anticlassicism) and Roman relief starting with the period of Marcus Aurelius, see P. Bober, *Drawings after the Antique by Amigo Aspertini*, pp. 27 and 38–39. Behind the beautiful and mysterious psychological separateness of figures in Peruzzi's *Presentation of the Virgin* or Pontormo's *Deposition* in Santa Felicita it is probably not too much to see, ultimately, the precedent of sarcophagi, as Anne Markham Goldenberg has stressed with relation to Peruzzi's picture in a colloquium at the Institute of Fine Arts shortly before this book went to press.

208. This would be a return to approximately what nineteenth century critics such as Burckhardt tended to think—although they did not label the anticipations Mannerism (see footnote 8)—but it would be a return in the light of an altered concept of *maniera*.

209. Even though Pontormo's picture retains from its model on Donatello's pulpit in San Lorenzo (see footnote 205 above) something of the latter's relief-like arrangement of figures.

Behind Donatello's *Christ before Pilate* lies more than medievalism, as Burger indicated when he credited the general character of Donatello's late relief style, as seen on the pulpits, to the influence of Roman relief, that of the Column of Trajan above all. (Fritz Burger, "Donatello und die Antike," *Repertorium für Kunstwissenschaft*, xxx, 1907, esp. pp. 2–9.) The view that Gothic is the background of the style is represented by W. R. Valentiner, *Studies of Italian Renaissance Sculpture*, London, 1950, pp. 1 ff. and G. Weise, "Donatello und das Problem der Spätgotik," *Zeitschrift für Kunstgeschichte*, XVII, 1954, pp. 79 ff. Lavin has shown how Donatello drew for the pulpits on both late medieval and antique sources, among the latter not simply Trajan's column, but other reliefs, including particularly sarcophagi. (I. Lavin, "The Sources of Donatello's Pulpits in San Lorenzo, Revival and Freedom of Choice in the Early Renaissance," *Art Bulletin*, XLI, 1959, pp. 19–38; *idem*, *The Sources of Donatello's Bronze Pulpits in San Lorenzo*, unpublished thesis, New York University, 1951, where the treatment of antique sources is fuller.) But Lavin did not mention again the antique aspects of Donatello's *Christ Before Pilate* when pointing to Donatello as Pontormo's source *(idem, An Observation on 'Medievalism' in Early Sixteenth Century Style)*.

In taking as his model a scene from Donatello's pulpits, where the style recalls even a sarcophagus like that cited in footnote 204 (it was known to the fifteenth century: see Krautheimer with Krautheimer-Hess, *Lorenzo Ghiberti*, pp. 341–342 and fig. 113), was Pontormo not reviving partly the antique aspect, though he made it much less recognizable? And in eliminating Donatello's space was he not making the scene conform more, in this respect, with Roman relief?

210. This is relevant to the question of whether Barocci's work is mannerist.

211. Above all, the main twentieth century concept of Mannerism seems to have a fascination of its own, which tends, I suspect, to keep us rather unswervingly interested in the spiritual, irrational, and expressionistic.

212. See Salmi, *La mostra del cinquecento toscano*, p. 83.

213. For this we owe some thanks to the preoccupation with Mannerism in its main twentieth century sense.

214. For doubts on the usefulness of the concept of Mannerism in the history of architecture, see James Ackerman, *The Architecture of Michelangelo*, London, 1961, I, p. xxii.

Corrigendum

Since this book went to press, I have grown doubtful about Naldini's authorship of the drawing reproduced in Figure 28. Philip Pouncey writes that he sympathizes with this hesitation although he had rather assumed it was by Naldini when he himself had connected it with the lunette in San Pierino, ten years ago. He thinks it is probably by an assistant, but not necessarily Balducci. The painting is difficult to see properly. While certainly in the style of Naldini, it might, I think, be largely an assistant's work. Meanwhile, Figures 12 and 27 will serve to illustrate the observation about Naldini made on page 24.

Plates

Fig. 1. Pontormo, *Christ before Pilate*. Florence, Certosa of Galluzzo (photo: Alinari).

(b) Vasari, *Immaculate Conception*. Lucca, Pinacoteca (photo: Alinari).

(a) Vasari, *Immaculate Conception*. Florence, SS. Apostoli (photo: Brogi).

Fig. 2.

Fig. 3. Bronzino, *Martyrdom of Saint Lawrence.* Florence, S. Lorenzo (photo: Alinari).

Fig. 5. Bronzino, *Saint John the Baptist*. Rome, Galleria Borghese (photo: Anderson).

Fig. 4. A. Allori, *Descent of Christ into Limbo*. Florence, S. Marco (photo: Brogi).

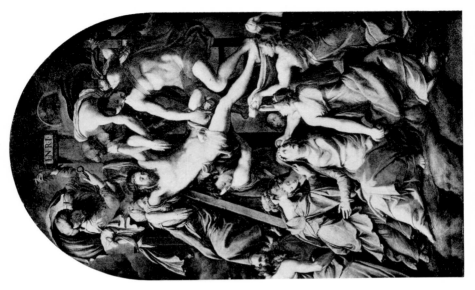

Fig. 7. Salviati, *Deposition*. Florence, S. Croce (photo: Alinari).

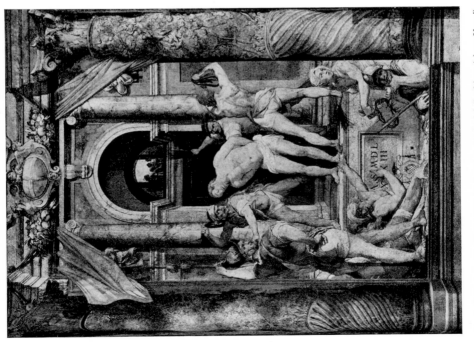

Fig. 6. F. Zuccaro, *Flagellation of Christ*. Rome, S. Lucia del Gonfalone (photo: Vasari).

Fig. 8. Poppi, *Christ Healing the Sick*. Florence ,S. Marco
(photo: Alinari)

Fig. 9. Vasari, *Pope Paul III Receives the Homage of the Nations*, Rome, Palazzo della Cancelleria
(photo: Anderson).

Fig. 10. A sampling of poses and gestures characteristic of *maniera* (photo: Smyth).

Fig. 11. Vasari School, Study for figures of the
Three Graces in preparation of the marriage of
Francesco de' Medici. Drawing. Florence, Uffizi,
no. 2785F (photo: Soprintendenza alle Gallerie).

Fig. 13. A. Allori, *Birth of the Virgin*. Florence, SS. Annunziata (photo: Brogi).

Fig. 12. Naldini, *Miracle of the Mama*.
Drawing, Florence, Uffizi, no. 713F (photo: Soprintendenza alle Gallerie).

Fig. 14. *Amazonomachy with Achilles and Penthesilea.* Rome, Villa Pamfili (photo: German Archaeological Institute, Rome).

Fig. 15. Battle Sarcophagus. Rome, Capitoline Museum (photo: Karl Lehmann).

Fig. 16. *Gigantomachy*, Vatican Museum (photo: Vatican).

Fig. 17. Season Sarcophagus, right section. New York, Metropolitan Museum of Art, purchase, 1955, Joseph Pulitzer Bequest (photo: Metropolitan Museum of Art).

Fig. 18. *Prometheus with the Gods*, Naples, National Museum (photo: Alinari).

Fig. 18. Vasari, *Siege of Pisa*. Florence, Palazzo Vecchio (photo: Brogi).

Fig. 20. Vasari, *Deposition*. Camaldoli (photo: Cipriani).

Fig. 21. (a) Bronzino, *Stigmatization of Saint Francis*. Florence, Palazzo Vecchio
(photo: Commune di Firenze).

(b) Bronzino, *Saint Michael*. Florence, Palazzo Vecchio (photo: Commune di Firenze).

Fig. 22. Bronzino, *Allegorical Figure*. Pesaro, Villa Imperiale
(photo: Smyth, by Pelosi, Ancona; courtesy Count Castelbarco Albani).

Fig. 23. Bronzino's design, *Allegorical
Figure*. Pesaro, Villa Imperiale
(photo: Smyth, by Felbermeyer;
courtesy Count Castelbarco Albani).

Fig. 24. Vasari, *Lorenzo the Magnificent and the Ambassadors.*
Drawing. Florence, Uffizi, no. 1185E
(photo: Soprintendenza alle Gallerie).

Fig. 25. Vasari, *Immaculate Conception.* Drawing. Florence,
Uffizi, no. 1181E (photo: Soprintendenza alle Gallerie).

Fig. 27. Naldini, *Adoration of the Child*.
Drawing. Florence, Uffizi, no. 705F (photo: Soprintendenza alle Gallerie).

Fig. 26. Vasari, *Immaculate Conception*.
Drawing. Florence, Uffizi, no. 1183E (photo: Soprintendenza alle Gallerie).

Fig. 28. Naldini, *Presentation*. Drawing. Florence, Uffizi, no. 9011S (photo: Soprintendenza alle Gallerie).

Fig. 29. Salviati, *Birth of the Virgin*. Rome, S. Marcello (photo: Vasari).

Fig. 30. Pontormo, *Last Judgment*. Drawing. Florence, Uffizi, no. 6609F
(photo: Soprintendenza alle Gallerie).

Fig. 31. El Greco, *Baptism*. Madrid, Prado (photo: Prado).

Fig. 32. Battle Sarcophagus (detail). Rome,
Galleria Borghese (photo: Felbermeyer).

Fig. 33. Pontormo, *Vertumnus and Pomona*. Poggio a Caiano (photo: Alinari).